how to decorate with wallpaper

how to
decorate
with
wallpaper

a practical and inspirational guide to using wallpaper

in the home, with step-by-step projects

Bernadette Fallon and Lauren Floodgate

NEW
HOLLAND

First published in 2007 by New Holland Publishers (UK) Ltd
London · Cape Town · Sydney · Auckland

Garfield House, 86–88 Edgware Road
London W2 2EA
United Kingdom
www.newhollandpublishers.com

80 McKenzie Street
Cape Town 8001
South Africa

Level 1, Unit 4, 14 Aquatic Drive
Frenchs Forest, NSW 2086
Australia

218 Lake Road
Northcote, Auckland
New Zealand

ISBN 978 1 84537 529 4

Senior Editor: Clare Sayer
Production: Hazel Kirkman
Design: The Bridgewater Book Company
Illustrations: Stephen Dew
Editorial Direction: Rosemary Wilkinson

10 9 8 7 6 5 4 3 2 1

Reproduction by Pica Digital (Pte) Ltd, Singapore
Printed and bound by Times Offset, Malaysia

CONTENTS

INTRODUCTION

Wallpaper is back and it's not difficult to see why. What other decorating tool is versatile enough to allow you to have fun with colours, tones, textures and depths, allowing you to add vivid or subtle shade and pattern to part of or a whole room?

Wallpapering is a job that can be accomplished by a total beginner – all you need is the correct know-how, and plenty of careful planning before you begin. This book will take you through everything you need to know to complete any wallpapering job successfully. If you've wallpapered before but want to brush up on your skills, you'll find great professional tips and designer inspiration to help improve your techniques and make the job easy.

Why wallpaper?

Using wallpaper is the ideal way to create a period feel or contemporary look, cosy up a large room or make small spaces feel bigger, add architectural interest to plain walls, create a rich enticing backdrop and highlight attractive features.

And not only that – wallpaper can also hide a multitude of sins, and is the perfect disguise for cracked walls or ceilings and uneven or bumpy surfaces. The right paper can add height to low ceilings, make narrow spaces feel wider and give a sense of depth to a shallow room.

Since the earliest drawings were scratched onto the surface of caves, we have used pattern and colour to decorate our living spaces, from wall frescos and hanging tapestries, through to the earliest wallpapers produced by hand at enormous effort and expense. From the superb craftsmanship of fine French papers to the delicate exotic designs of the Far East and China, from the formal Colonial style of post Revolution America to the English Renaissance of William Morris, from the flowering of Art Deco styles right down to the lavish profusion of bright colour and pattern of the decadent swinging '60s and '70s, wallpaper has continued to evolve with the times.

Wallpaper today

With contemporary technology the range of choice continues to grow, from eye-catching large-scale digital prints to a great variety of faux finishes such as leather, brick and stone – no other design tool offers such an amazing array of choices to indulge your creative passion, no matter what your personal design style.

All price brackets are catered for, so whether you are trying to decorate on a tight budget or splashing out on a luxurious option, you'll find something to suit you.

▶ **right** Horizontal stripes make a narrow room appear wider

▶ **far right** A bold pattern with a large recurring motif creates a striking feature wall

How it all began

Wall decoration dates back to the time of Egyptian and Roman wall painting, and evolved through to the lavish tapestries used to adorn the walls of European castles and palaces. The first wallpaper is believed to date back to the fifteenth century as a substitute for these costly wall hangings, though historians also claim the first wallpaper – a form of rice paper – was being used in Chinese homes as early as 200 BC!

In the late 1400s Louis XI of France commissioned sheets of paper to decorate his palace from a French craftsman who presented him with a design of angels on a blue background – however Louis specified that this paper must be portable, as he moved frequently from castle to castle. In fact the earliest forms of wallpaper were not hung on the walls at all, but instead were pasted onto linen, which was then attached to the walls with metal tacks. Wallpaper borders were originally developed as a clever way to hide the tacks from view.

Invention of wallpaper

However, the inventor of wallpaper as we know it today is considered to be a French engraver, Jean-Michel Papillon, who started to make matching continuous block designs on paper in the late 1600s.

The focus moved to England in the 1700s as manufacturing methods became more sophisticated and the papers produced in London workshops became highly fashionable. Chinese papers were also imported and proved very popular. Wallpaper came to the US in the mid 1700s, and the first wallpaper was printed in Philadelphia. At first American designs copied their European forerunners, but post Revolution American workshops created their own styles and looks, many depicting patriotic 'commemorative' scenes.

The first machine for printing wallpaper was invented in the later part of the 18th century in France. The early decades of the 1800s saw the English develop the process further to create high-speed colour printing machines.

Advances in technology

With the new technology, wallpaper manufacture really came into its own, and wallpaper became hugely popular in Victorian and Edwardian homes. As production increased, prices dropped so more and more people could afford it for their homes.

William Morris further developed its popularity in the pre-Raphaelite period in Britain, and his designs are still widely drawn on today. However, the golden age of wallpaper is not considered to have taken place until the 1920s, when some 400 million rolls of paper were sold worldwide.

Popularity of papers continued to rise and fall throughout the decades of the 20th century, reaching a peak in the pattern-rich world of interiors in the 1960s and '70s. The austere minimalist fashions of the closing decades of the 20th century saw a return to bare walls however, and it was not until the new millennium – a new design era with a strong focus on individualism – that wallpaper returned to its popular position as a creative and innovative design tool.

◀ **left** A modern take on a traditional floral print is ideal for a contemporary space

◀ **left** A recurring motif adds dramatic impact and is ideal for a feature wall

How to use this book

How to Decorate with Wallpaper is your complete guide to wallpapering with confidence and ease for professional and lasting results every time. Within these pages you'll find everything you need to know about wallpaper – from choosing to planning to hanging, and much more! The book is divided into comprehensive sections for easy reference.

Essentials

Wallpaper Essentials covers all the basic information you need to get you started, with chapters on style and colour advice, choosing the right type of paper, calculating the right amount to buy, finding out what tools you'll need, how to prepare surfaces correctly and a list of common problems and pitfalls to avoid. You'll learn how to match different types of paper to the different rooms in your house, how to work effectively with the huge variety of colours, patterns, finishes and styles on offer, with insider tips from the professionals. The how-to guides in this section are detailed in easy to follow step-by-step projects – here's where you'll learn how to paper an entire room, both walls and ceiling.

Projects

Wallpaper Projects offers a greater level of detail on tackling all those tricky bits, such as papering around corners, papering around windows and doors, and dealing with obstacles such as radiators and light switches.

As well as these highly detailed practical projects, there are also style projects that cover more complicated design issues such as hanging two or more different papers in one room, working with stickers, how to use stripes and borders in a design scheme and making the most of a feature wall with wallpaper.

Glossary

There's a full glossary at the back of all the terms used throughout this book – use it for quick and easy reference if there's anything you need to clarify as you work through the chapters.

Getting started

Make the most of all the information within this book, and use it to make your own personal choices about what works best for you. Don't rush out and buy the first paper you see. Take your time, do your research, study all of the options available to you before making your purchase.

Plan the job carefully before you start, make sure you have invested in all the correct tools and that you have allowed enough time to complete the job without interruption. Remember, you will have to live with the results you achieve and any mistakes could be very costly. But above all, have fun creating inspiring spaces that will continue to give you pleasure in the years to come.

wallpaper essentials

Whether you are a complete novice or looking to improve your skills, this section provides everything you need to know to tackle the job of wallpapering with confidence and ease from start to finish.

From the planning stages, with useful information on choosing the right type of paper, making informed colour choices and pattern matching, to knowing how much paper to buy and what tools you will need, right down to the big job itself – wallpapering rooms and ceilings, this section takes you through it all.

Equip yourself with all the necessary know-how before you begin – and you can't go wrong!

TOOLS AND MATERIALS

A good start is half the battle. Investing in the correct materials and tools is vital before you begin wallpapering – it will make the job easier and, remember, these tools will see you through many projects in years to come. Use our checklist to ensure you are adequately prepared to start work.

Materials

Wallpaper – see 'Tips before you shop'
Paste to suit the paper and wall covering
Sugar soap to clean walls before papering
Primer-sealer to prepare new walls for papering

Tips before you shop

Every roll of paper is identified by a batch number – also referred to as the dye lot, run or shade number. All rolls with the same number carry the same shade and ink qualities. While the pattern may be the same on rolls carrying a different number, the ink does not always take to the paper in the same way, which means you can end up with dramatic differences in shade. For this reason it is important to buy all papers with the same batch numbers to avoid colour variations. Also, before you start, look closely at the rolls to make sure they are the same shade – it's too late once the paper has been hung!

Tools and equipment

Preparation
Dust sheets
Decorator's apron
Cork block and glass paper, or sanding block
Fine mist garden sprayer – to moisten paper for easy removal
Stepladder with platform top for safety
Stripping knife – to remove old paper
Sponge – for cleaning walls

Pasting and hanging
Measuring tape
Ruler – 600 mm (24 in)
Spirit level – 900 mm (35 in)
Masking tape
Soft pencil
Straight edge
Pasting table
Two buckets – for paste and water
Clean stick or wooden spoon – for stirring paste
Paste brush
Plumb bob and chalk
Paperhanging bristle brush
Paperhanger's scissors
Seam roller
Damp cloth – to clean paste from skirting
Broad blade knife
Trimming knife with snap-off blades

Extras

Overlap paste – for vinyl paper
Water tray – for pre-pasted paper
Felt wallpaper roller – for moulded, flock or delicate hand printed papers
Lining paper – for use under certain types of paper or on uneven walls
Smoothing brush
Paste roller, if using 'paste the wall' paper
Steam stripper, to help remove old paper
Two trestles and two scaffold boards – for papering ceilings
Safety goggles – if using steam stripper on ceilings
Four large bulldog clips – to hold paper in place if cutting several strips at once

Good idea

Remember you may have to make repairs in the future, so keep a roll of paper handy after the job is done. If you run out, at least keep a record of the wallpaper manufacturer and the batch numbers – you may be able to order additional rolls at a later stage, though there are no guarantees!

▼ **below** The basic equipment you need for wallpapering, clockwise from centre: spirit level, tape measure, paste brush, paperhanging brush, bucket, wooden spoon, wallpaper, sponge, plumb bob, seam roller, paperhanging scissors, trimming knife, pencil, decorator's apron, pasting table

TYPES OF PAPER

Not only are there a huge number of colours, designs and styles to choose from when buying your wallpaper, there are also many different types of paper to consider. When choosing what is best for you, take into account the room size and use, and your level of skill, as well as your personal taste. Certain types of paper are better suited to beginners than others – leave metallic papers until you have refined your wallpapering skills a little!

▲ **above** The raised finish of elegant Lincrusta is an ideal surface for painting over

Lincrusta

Traditionally used in hallways or as a frieze in formal living spaces, this heavy wall covering dates from the 1800s and features a raised design surface with the texture of hard putty. It should be hung with a special clay-based paint and can be finished with paint or glaze.

When hanging Lincrusta, first sponge the back of the strip with hot water until thoroughly soaked. Paste, then hang the length as normal. Rub down after with a felt or sponge roller. Always cut using a sharp craft knife and a straight edge. Cut to fit into corners and fill gaps at external corners with a decorator's filler.

Ease of hanging: This paper is very heavy and requires a slightly different hanging technique. Unless you are a very experienced DIYer it is best left to the professionals.

Good for: Period homes, elegant living spaces, formal rooms.

Toile de Jouy

This highly decorative engraving-like print originated in 18th century France and is named for its birth city outside Paris – the name literally means 'cloth of Jouy'. Traditionally comprising landscape and figure motifs in shades of muted colours on a plain background, it adds a pretty feminine touch to living areas or bedrooms.

Ease of hanging: Must be very carefully matched and so requires accurate hanging.

Good for: Both modern and traditional settings, creating an eye-catching feature wall.

◀ **left** Metallic wallpapers are a great way to add glamour to a room, particularly with a bold retro print

Metallic

Metallic paper – also referred to as foil – is exactly what the name suggests, a paper with a metallic sheen that looks like real metal. It is the perfect way to brighten up a dark area or create a spacious feeling in smaller rooms. If you like the look, but are not adventurous enough to opt for a whole room in this effect, keep to a feature wall or alcove, or choose a standard paper with metallic motifs.

Ease of hanging: Can show imperfections if not hung very accurately and so it is not ideal for a beginner.

Good for: The reflective surfaces will make small rooms feel bigger and brighten up dark rooms – however walls should be free of surface imperfections for best effect.

Flock

A highly decorative paper with a velvet pile bonded onto its surface, flock creates an eye-catching effect that is ideal for formal rooms and more traditional design schemes.

It is important not to allow any paste onto the surface of the paper when hanging, as it is almost impossible to remove paste from flocking. Protect the surface with a piece of thin lining paper, and apply the paper with a clean brush or felt roller.

Ease of hanging: This pattern requires careful matching, making it one of the more difficult options.

Good for: Traditional room schemes, adding warmth to a room.

Textured

This paper has a raised pattern for a rich warm effect and tactile appeal. It is generally suitable for painting afterwards, either to add a new dimension to the scheme, or for freshening up tired walls. Textured paper is also a great way to add warmth to a painted room when used on a feature wall or chimney breast.

◀ **left** A traditional flock wallpaper looks great in a formal setting

Ease of hanging: This type of paper can be quite fragile so take care when hanging.

Good for: Adding texture to plain surfaces, hiding surface imperfections on walls and ceilings.

Stickers

Stickers are a great way to add interest, introduce pattern and colour or create a theme on painted or papered walls. They come in a huge variety of designs and are especially good for children's rooms. Many can also be repositioned if you tire of the layout, as they peel off the wall easily. Ensure surfaces are flat, clean and dry before applying.

Ease of hanging: Good – self-adhesive stickers simply peel and stick.

Good for: Children's rooms and nurseries, adding colour and pattern to plain rooms.

Leather

Real leather wallpaper is thought to date back to 17th-century Italy, and was also very popular in Victorian England. Today imitation leather wall covering is also available, and looks amazingly like the real thing. Advanced technology has also enabled production of coverings that are a perfect imitation of wood, stone, brick and cork. Some finishes can also be painted once hung.

▶ **right** Available in a huge range of colours, styles and designs, stickers are a great way of brightening up a room

Ease of hanging: Not suitable for inexperienced DIYers.

Good for: Adding warmth to a room, making a statement.

Embossed

With its raised and textured pattern, embossed papers include Anaglypta and Lincrusta, though lighter options are easier to hang than these more specialist designs. Patterns are generally geometric and eye-catching, good for traditional rooms and period schemes. Embossed paper can also be painted once hung – this is a particularly good idea for freshening up a tired room scheme. Its textured style also makes it ideal for use on ceilings.

Ease of hanging: While it is not particularly difficult to hang, embossed paper needs to be handled with care to avoid flattening the pattern, particularly when butting strips together and turning corners.

Good for: Hiding uneven surfaces.

◀ **left** The luxurious look of leather creates warmth and makes a statement

Other options

Lining paper Used underneath to give a smooth base and better adhesion when hanging expensive wallcoverings, it is also ideal for covering up surface imperfections that cannot be easily patched by filler. When used as a base it should be hung horizontally so the joins don't match up with those in the top layer of paper. It can also be hung vertically and painted over. It is available in different grades for different requirements. While a lightweight paper is fine for most standard wallpapering jobs, if you are hanging lining paper with a view to painting over it, choose a heavier grade.

Vinyl A tough, hardwearing plastic-coated paper, which is washable and particularly suited for kitchens and bathrooms. Bear in mind though, it can be more difficult to remove. When hanging vinyl you will need to use a specially formulated 'vinyl to vinyl' adhesive along any overlaps, as vinyl will not stick to itself.

Vinyl coated With a thin skin of plastic, this paper is easier to remove than standard vinyl and its protective surface covering also makes it suitable for kitchens and bathrooms.

Washable A thin plastic coating makes this paper more resistant to stains and marks, as it can be regularly wiped down.

Scrubbable Stronger than washable, this paper will withstand more vigorous cleaning and is ideal for areas of high traffic such as hallways or children's rooms.

'Cloth' papers Reminiscent of early wallcoverings made from grasscloth, linen, silk and wool, modern versions are manufactured with a durable paper backing for easy hanging. In addition, modern printing methods make it easy to recreate the look of these materials using paper or vinyl for a more durable covering.

Hand printed Not very widely available these days, this type of paper is very expensive and should only be hung by professional decorators.

▲ **above** Use an embossed paper to hide uneven surfaces and add texture

▲ **above** Elegant stripes create a feeling of symmetry and balance

WHAT TO USE WHERE

The type of paper you select will obviously be heavily influenced by your personal taste but there are many other factors you should also take into consideration when making your choice. The right paper will maximize the potential of a room, hide its shortcomings and be perfectly suited to the purpose and function of the space.

◄ **left** A reflective metallic paper creates a contemporary look when used all over a room

wipe down. Washable and scrubbable designs are best for children's rooms and any other areas where spills and stains might be a problem.

You can probably indulge your personal taste and pay less attention to practical matters like durability when it comes to choosing wallpaper for private areas in adult's bedrooms, studies and dens. But again, think carefully. A bright design may look great in a bedroom, but will it help you sleep?

Delicate papers such as grass and fabric cloths are best saved for 'show' rooms and rooms that are not subject to a large degree of wear and tear. Likewise for expensive hand printed papers. Generally, the price of a paper will often dictate its place within the home, as you will not want to hang papers that are easily damaged in busy, high traffic areas such as hallways and kitchens.

Choosing: the basics

When choosing paper there are a number of important questions to consider.

First, define the room's function, use and traffic levels. 'Show' rooms such as the entrance hallway, living and dining room should be warm, welcoming and stylish; however the hallway, like the kitchen and family room, is also a high traffic area so the covering chosen should be durable and easy to maintain.

Wallpaper in bathrooms needs to be able to withstand water splashes and humidity, while wallpaper in kitchens will also be subjected to a high degree of wear and tear, as will the coverings in a children's bedroom.

Vinyl and vinyl-coated papers are tough, hardwearing papers, which are ideal for kitchens and bathrooms. A plastic coated finish makes it easy to

Choosing: the room

Now take stock of the room itself, analyzing the space carefully and looking at:

- Assets and liabilities – are there areas to highlight or problems to be disguised?
- Size and shape – is the room narrow, square, L-shaped?
- Windows – how many, are they large or small, awkwardly placed or shaped?
- Ceiling – is it too high or low, are there mouldings to work around?
- Architectural features – does the room have fireplaces, mouldings, alcoves or archways? Are these assets to highlight or obstacles to negotiate?

◄ **left** An eye-catching pattern is ideal for a 'show' room or one that isn't used on a daily basis, such as a dining room

▲ **above** Light-absorbing colours, such as rich oranges will create a warm atmosphere that may not suit every room

Design tricks

As well as practical considerations, there are a number of design tricks that can be called into use to make the most of a room, no matter how uninspiring or awkward it may first seem.

• Use a horizontal pattern to make a room seem wider, a great way to 'extend' the width of narrow rooms or short feature walls. Bear in mind though, if your walls and ceiling are not square or true, a horizontal pattern will draw attention to this fact.

• A vertical pattern makes the ceiling in a room look higher and is an excellent choice for a room with a low ceiling – geometrical patterns such as stripes, plaids and checks all work well.

• Choose a drop pattern to hide the fact your room isn't perfectly square or true. But remember that this pattern, repeated diagonally across the strip, will require additional paper to match up.

• Light colours and small prints create a feeling of space – great for small rooms. A light-reflecting or metallic paper will also open up a small space and make it feel bigger and more luxurious.

• Large prints and darker shades cosy up a large room and add warmth. Light-absorbing colours such as rich earthy golds, reds and terracotta will create an intimate atmosphere.

WORKING WITH PATTERN AND COLOUR

Colour is important in any decorating scheme – to set the mood, suggest a style, make rooms look bigger or more intimate and create a perfect atmosphere. Wallpaper has the added advantage of introducing not only colour but also pattern and texture to a room, and the effects you can achieve are only limited by your imagination.

The position of colours on the colour wheel gives an indication of how they will work together. Contrasting schemes, such as purple and orange, combine shades on opposite sides of the wheel for a dramatic effect. Harmonious schemes, such as green and blue, work with colours beside each other to create a fresh tranquil look. Tonal schemes combine several shades of one colour for a look that is easy on the eye.

With so many colours and styles to choose from, it's easy to feel overwhelmed. A mood board is a very useful tool to help develop your personal design style. It's easy to do – just collect examples of colour combinations, styles, patterns and looks that appeal to you using colour cards, wallpaper and fabric swatches, pictures from magazines, postcards and anything else that inspires you, to build up your own individual style. Eventually a pattern will emerge and you have the basic template for putting your own look together, using the key patterns, colours and styles you are drawn to.

Design basics

Knowledge of the basic design tools employed widely by interior designers and stylists will help you create your own perfect decorating scheme.

The colour wheel (see right) shows the relationship between different colours. All colours are created from the three primary colours of blue, red and yellow. Cool colours sit on the blue side of the wheel – their receding qualities make spaces feel bigger. Warm colours on the red and yellow side appear to advance, making a room seem cosy but smaller.

▲ **above** Wallpaper is the ideal way to add colour, pattern and texture to a room

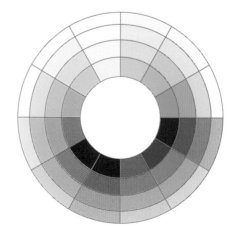

▶ **right** Mixing two different patterns in a room scheme can work to stunning effect

Making it work

While personal choice will play a large part in making your selections, there are certain tricks to follow to make the most of colour and pattern in any space.

- Large patterns work best in large spaces, where there is enough wall area to see the pattern repeated. You can afford to play with scale and be bold in a large room by introducing an oversized pattern. Large prints have a big impact on the mood of a room and add excitement, drama and visual interest.
- Small prints have a tendency to get lost in large rooms but work very well in smaller spaces where the detail can be appreciated. Keep colours light in small rooms to make the space feel bigger, a small repeated print will also create a spacious feeling rather than a bold pattern which make the walls seem closer.
- If you have fallen in love with a brightly coloured pattern but are worried it will be too overpowering in a room, use it on a feature wall to make an impact. Keep the other walls neutral for best effect, or pick up one of the colours in the pattern and paint the rest of the room in this shade.
- A tonal scheme, where all colours are variations of the same shade has the effect of making a room seem bigger, as the eye is able to move through the room uninterrupted, creating an illusion of additional space. Using a widely spaced pattern such as diamonds or mid-sized flowers with lots of white space in between will have the same effect, and give an airy, open feeling to the room.
- To cosy up a large room and make it feel more inviting, use a large print and darker, light-absorbing colours. Use rich colours like deep red, gold and aubergine in rooms with northern exposure or with limited sunlight to add warmth.
- Use dark colours and intricate patterns on high ceilings to make them feel lower; lighter colours and subtle motifs to make low ceilings feel higher.

Around the house

Colours for hallways should be bright and welcoming, hallways are also a great place to introduce bold patterns that might be too busy for a room you spend more time in.

Living rooms work best with more restful patterns that are easy on the eye unless you have a very large room – however a bold pattern can really offset a neutral scheme if used on a feature wall or to highlight an alcove or recess. Another idea is to make use of a dado rail to display coordinating papers, which gives more scope to play around with colour and pattern.

A bedroom will also benefit from a subtle palette that aids rest and relaxation, though you can of course introduce bright colours and patterns as accents around the room, or consider matching a dramatic paper with a more subtle design on adjoining walls.

A separate dining room is often quite a formal space that suits a geometric pattern like stripes and plaids; warm colours that stimulate appetite also work well.

Warm colours also look best in a kitchen where the family spends a lot of time, small prints and motifs such as fruits, leaves and flowers are also a popular choice here.

Using different papers to add texture is also a great idea in an L-shaped room, or to suggest subtle divisions in a large multi-functional room such as an office space within a living room, a dining area in a kitchen, or a play zone in a child's bedroom.

WORKING WITH PATTERN AND COLOUR

Good tip

If you plan to hang a lot of artwork, textiles or other decorative objects it's best to keep walls fairly neutral to prevent the pattern competing and to provide an effective backdrop. White, cream, beige and soft grey will all work well, to add a touch more colour opt for sand, stone, biscuit or pale pastels.

◄ **left** A floral print in delicate shades adds a soft feminine touch – the bold design is offset by the subtle colours

◄ **far left** This brightly coloured floral print is perfect as a feature wall in a pretty bathroom

Key to success

Successful decorating schemes do not employ more than three key colours. Contrary to what you may think, using pattern in your scheme makes choosing a colour scheme easy as most patterns combine colours that work very well together.

Do not over-mix pattern, the best decorated rooms do not contain more than three or, at most, four different patterns in fabrics and wall coverings. To ensure that patterns work well together, opt for those that have a common element such as motifs and colours. There is nothing wrong with combining stripes, checks and florals, as long as there is balance in scale and some common colours to provide balance.

Linking spaces

Think about how your design scheme will relate to connecting spaces, between a hallway and living room for example, or a living room that leads into a dining room. You may wish to pick up common colours or pattern motifs between interlinked spaces, to give a harmonious feel.

Choose papers from the same paper family to create an overall design scheme that blends easily without repetition. Check out pattern books at wallpaper stores – papers that complement each other sit together in these books to make choosing easier.

BUYING WALLPAPER

When it comes to buying your paper, there are two vital things to get right; first that you buy enough paper to complete the job and second you buy the correct paper to suit the room you are papering.

The first is a simple calculation – use these formulas and table to make it easy. Bear in mind however that the number of rolls you will need to buy depends on the pattern repeat. To keep costs down choose a non-matching paper or a design with a random match, which will result in less wastage.

Choosing the right paper depends on a variety of factors including skill level, room use and size, maintenance, etc. All of the information you need can be obtained from the individual rolls of paper – the table of wallpaper symbols opposite will ensure you get it right with no costly mistakes.

Calculating how much paper to buy

You don't want to stop short three feet from the edge of the room – remember, you may not be able to match the correct paper at a later stage. Get it right first time.

Calculating wall area to be covered

To find the total wall area of the room you are papering, first measure the length of all the walls, add together and multiply by the height of the walls.

L x H = Total area

Next measure doors and windows, calculate the area covered in the same way as above, and subtract this number from the total area.

Door area + window area
= Door and window area

Total area – Door and window area
= Total wall area to be covered

How many rolls?

Wallpaper is sold in single, double and triple rolls – the wallpaper label will include details of the area covered in square metres or feet. Once you have chosen a paper, divide that figure into the total square wall area of the room you are papering. The number you get (round up decimals to the nearest whole number) will be the number of rolls you need to buy.

$$\frac{\text{Total wall area}}{\text{Area covered by one roll}} = \text{Number of rolls needed, plus one for wastage}$$

Use the chart opposite as a guide to estimate how much paper you will need for different sized rooms. But remember, the number of rolls required will vary according to pattern and room shape. Always allow an extra roll for wastage.

Good tip

If you overestimate and buy too much wallpaper, some stores will allow you to return unopened rolls for a full refund – check before you buy.

Be careful

You should always add at least one extra roll for wastage, more if using paper with a large pattern.

Lining paper

If you hanging lining paper as a base to paper over, you should hang it horizontally so that the joins do not line up in the top layer. This means that room height is less of a factor as you will require less lining paper. Use the chart below, but remember, it is intended only as a guide.

DISTANCE AROUND THE ROOM	NUMBER OF ROLLS
8.5 m (27¾ ft)	1
12.1 m (39¾ ft)	2
14.6 m (48 ft)	3
17.6 m (57¾ ft)	4
20 m (65½ ft)	5
21.2 m (69½ ft)	6
23.7 m (77¾ ft)	7
25 m (82 ft)	8
26 m (85¼ ft)	9
26.8 m (88 ft)	10
30.5 m (100 ft)	12

Important note

If you plan to use lining paper as a base to paint over, then you should hang it vertically, as with standard paper. To calculate how much you will need in this case, see the chart above.

Wallpaper symbols

Do you want washable, strippable, fade resistant or free match? Our handy guide takes you through the standard wallpaper symbols, so you know you are buying exactly what you need.

Wallpaper

AT A GLANCE GUIDE	WALL HEIGHT FROM SKIRTING			
DISTANCE AROUND THE ROOM	2 m (7 ft)	2.5m (8 ft)	2.7 m (9 ft)	3 m (10 ft)
9 m (30 ft)	4	5	5	6
10 m (34 ft)	5	5	5	6
12 m (38 ft)	5	6	6	7
13 m (42 ft)	6	6	7	8
14 m (46 ft)	6	7	7	8
15 m (50 ft)	7	7	8	9
16 m (54 ft)	7	8	9	10
17 m (58 ft)	8	8	9	10
19 m (62 ft)	8	9	10	11
20 m (66 ft)	9	9	10	12
21 m (70 ft)	9	10	11	12
22 m (74 ft)	10	10	12	13
24 m (78 ft)	10	11	12	14
25 m (82 ft)	11	11	13	14
26 m (86 ft)	12	12	14	15
27 m (90 ft)	12	13	14	16
29 m (94 ft)	13	13	15	16
30 m (98 ft)	13	14	15	17

Symbol		Symbol	
Spongeable at time of hanging		Offset match	
Washable		Reverse alternate lengths	
Extra washable		To be hung horizontally	
Scrubbable		Adhesive to be applied to the wallcovering	
Extra scrubbable		Adhesive to be applied to the wall	
Moderate colour fastness to light		Prepasted (ready pasted)	
Good colour fastness to light		Strippable	
Excellent colour fastness to light		Peelable	
Free match		Wet removable	
Straight match			

PREPARING FOR PAPERING AND CROSS LINING

No matter how much care you take with your papering, if you don't prepare the surfaces adequately before you begin, you won't achieve a professional finish. If hanging embossed or expensive coverings, or papering over a surface that is not fully smooth, you will need to cross line the wall or ceiling first with lining paper to create a good base on which to work.

Preparing surfaces

Preparing surfaces properly not only means your paper will go up easier, it will also make stripping it easier when the time comes for removal. Always make sure that walls are clean, dry and sound before you start to paper.

Painted or plastered surfaces

Fill in holes and repair any damaged plaster with a fine surface filler. Allow to dry, then sand smooth using medium-grade sandpaper. Wash thoroughly with sugar soap to remove all loose paint and plaster.

If the surface has been gloss painted, rub it down with 40-grit abrasive paper wrapped around a cork block – for convenience – or else use a sanding block, which can be purchased from any DIY shop.

If preparing newly plastered surfaces, you may need to cover with a coat of primer-sealer to prevent the paste soaking right into the wall, making removal extremely difficult.

Papered surfaces

Stripping wallpaper can be a messy job so cover the floor with dustsheets and either move furniture out or keep it covered in the centre of the room. Moisten the paper as you work using a solution of warm water and washing up detergent applied with a brush or fine-mist garden sprayer.

Apply the water from the bottom up and remove paper with a stripping knife. Stubborn patches will need extra soaking. Painted paper may also need scoring with a sharp knife before soaking – be careful not to damage the wall underneath however.

Once all the paper has been removed repair any holes or cracks with filler, and sand smooth when dry. Wash the walls thoroughly with sugar soap before you start to paper.

Steam stripping

Investing in a professional wallpaper steam stripper will greatly speed up the job, and is especially useful for removing paper that has been painted. Steam strippers and perforators are also available for hire – they are not expensive and really make light work of what can otherwise be a difficult task. A perforator is designed to work in conjunction wtih a steam stripper, with sharp spikes to pierce the paper. It allows the steam to penetrate more easily. If stripping paper off hard-to-reach areas like staircases and high landings, you should also consider hiring scaffolding for ease of reach and safety.

Safety tips

Take extra care when using a steam stripper on ceilings as it can spit out hot water. Always hold it in front of you, never directly overhead, and always wear safety goggles and long sleeves.

Open windows when using a steam stripper to diffuse the steam – otherwise it is difficult to see what you are doing.

Cross lining

Lining paper should be used as a base for embossed or expensive wallcoverings – it is also ideal for covering up surface imperfections that cannot be easily patched by filler. Hang it horizontally so the joins don't match up with those in the top layer of paper. If you plan to paint over your lining paper you should hang it vertically as you would normal paper. When cross lining a ceiling, hang it at a 90-degree angle to the finished covering to prevent the edges of the papers running in the same direction.

1 Use a spirit level and pencil to mark a horizontal line on the wall, one roll width down from where you intend to start papering – either the ceiling or picture rail.

2 Cut as many lengths as you need to cover one wall, cutting each one 100 mm (4 in) longer than you need. Place all the lengths face down, reverse side up on the pasting table.

3 Mix wallpaper paste in a bucket according to the packet instructions, which should also include information on the strength and amount of paste needed for the type of paper you are hanging.

4 Apply the paste to the top length, starting at one end and working your way down to the other, pasting from the middle out to the edges so that the paper doesn't lift and peel after it is hung (**diagram A**). As you paste, fold the paper into a loose concertina but do not crease.

5 Allow paper to soak according to instructions. Pick up folded paper by its top edge and, starting in the corner, line up the bottom edge of the paper with the pencil line. Smooth onto the wall with the papering brush (**diagram B**), working from the centre out towards the edges with a sweeping motion, making sure there are no air bubbles (**diagram C**). Work along the wall, unfolding the length as you go without stretching or tearing. It is best to work with two people, so that one can support the paper while the other fixes it on the wall.

6 Using the top of the brush, gently stipple or tap the paper into the corners. To trim, mark a line down the corner of the paper with the bristle brush, ease the paper away from the wall and cut with scissors. Brush back into place. Trim in the same way at ceiling and skirting level (**diagram D**).

7 Before hanging the second length, paste the third to allow it to soak. Butt up each length of paper to the one before, working down the wall. Ensure there is no overlap at the joins as this will spoil the finish of the outside paper. Wipe away the paste as you work to prevent stains or marks showing on the paper's surface.

8 Allow to dry for 24 hours before covering.

A Apply paste to the paper

B Smooth onto the wall

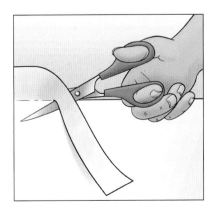

C Work out towards the edges

D Trim at skirting

WALLPAPERING A ROOM

Wallpapering a whole room is a job that requires skill and patience, though once armed with the necessary know-how it is a job that can be successfully completed by a beginner. And just think how proud you'll be when people admire your handiwork. Bear in mind though, that while it is a job that can be undertaken alone it is often much easier with two people.

Getting started

1 First move all furniture away from the walls and into the centre of the room, ensuring this leaves enough space for you to set up your pasting table and to work comfortably. Remove fixtures like curtain poles, outlet covers and switch plates – for information on papering around obstacles see page 52–55.

2 Mix wallpaper paste in a bucket according to the packet instructions, which should also include information on the strength and amount of paste needed for the type of paper you are hanging.

Good tip

Tie a piece of thick string across the top of your bucket – an ideal place to rest the bristles of your brush to keep them clean of excess paste, stop paste dripping onto the floor and prevent the brush dropping into the bucket.

◀ **left** Wallpapering a room is not difficult but a professional result takes patience and know-how

3 Measure the height of your wall to find out how long each strip of wallpaper should be. Because wall height may vary around the room – particularly in older houses – it is advisable to take this measurement at a few points around the room, then use the maximum measurement. Now add about 100 mm (4 in) to this measurement, to allow for trimming at ceiling and skirting board level.

Finding your starting point

1 It is essential to make the right decision when it comes to hanging your first strip of paper. This will be determined by a number of factors. Patterned papers look best with the pattern

Good tip

For patterned paper you may have to allow extra for pattern matching on adjacent strips, and you may find it works better to cut strips from alternate rolls as you work. For more on working with patterned paper, see pages 32–34.

A Using a plumb bob

centred on a focal wall. This may be a chimney breast or the wall you see first when you enter the room. If the room has a feature such as an archway, this may be the best place to start.

2 If your room does not have any features, start papering on a wall that has neither door nor window, beginning at one corner and moving away from the window.

3 Whatever you decide to do, it is essential to plan your route around the room before you start and stick to it.

Using a plumb bob

1 As walls are rarely completely straight or 'true plumb' you need to mark a straight vertical line on the wall with a plumb bob. Use this as a guideline to hang your first strip. Mark a new plumb line every time you turn a corner.

2 Mark your starting position on the wall close to the ceiling, and less than one roll width away from the corner. Fix the end of the plumb line over this mark with masking tape. Allow the weight to hang freely and steady it. Make several pencil lines along the string and join these marks with a ruler to complete the vertical line from top to bottom. Alternatively, rub the string of the plumb line with chalk and, once it has steadied, hold it to the wall at the bottom and 'snap' the string. This will leave a vertical chalk line on the wall (**diagram A**).

Cutting

1 Use paperhanger's scissors to cut your first strip of paper to the length determined. Wait until you have hung the first strip to cut subsequent lengths – this will ensure you are cutting to the correct measurement. If working with two people you can use the 'hung' strip to measure subsequent lengths – just hold the roll next to the pasted strip on the wall when matching and cutting the second length.

Pasting

1 Place the first strip reverse side up on the pasting table. Line up the end and side edge of the wallpaper strip with the end and side edge of the pasting table, and paste from the centre of the paper to the edge for the whole length of the table. Make sure all edges are well covered (**diagram A**).

2 Carefully fold over the pasted length and pull the unpasted length onto the table. Paste as before and fold over to meet in the centre so that both pasted sides of the paper are together (**diagram B**). Don't flatten the ends of the folds. This is referred to as 'booking' the paper.

3 Remove from the table and leave to 'soak' if required by the manufacturer's pasting instructions. This is generally only necessary for heavyweight papers.

▲ **above** Create a unified design scheme with matching wallpaper and curtains

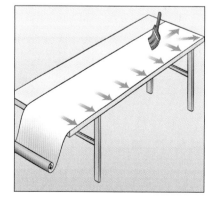

A Paste out from the centre

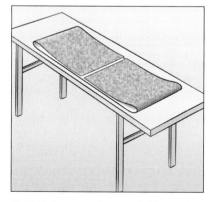

B Fold the paper to meet in the centre

Hanging

1 Unfold the top half of the pasted length and press it gently against the top of the wall, aligning it neatly on one side with the plumb line – remember to leave enough surplus at the top for trimming (**diagram A**). Smooth the paper into position, starting at the top and working down, brushing outwards diagonally with your wallpaper brush to smooth paper and remove air bubbles, keeping a check that the paper is correctly aligned with the plumb line all the way down. Unfold the bottom half and brush into place using the same method.

2 Crease the paper into the angles between the wall, ceiling and skirting board using the back edge of the scissors or bristle brush, then peel back the paper and trim along the creases. Smooth back into position with the brush. Alternatively, the excess can be trimmed with a sharp trimming knife. If using this method, wait until you have hung a few strips and trim them all at once to save time.

3 Wipe off any excess paste from the ceiling, skirting and surface of the paper using a clean damp cloth or sponge (**diagram B**). Now hang the next strip, moving in the direction you have already plotted out, making sure the edge butts up neatly to the edge of the first strip without overlapping or leaving a gap. Slide the paper gently into position – if you are unhappy with the 'fit', carefully remove the strip and reapply. Take care to match the pattern if the paper has one.

4 When the paper is nearly dry, smooth the joins between the strips with a seam roller (**diagram C**). Be careful not to over-roll as this may force the adhesive to the surface, which will then get wiped away causing edges to lift. Do not roll seams on flocks, foils, fabrics or embossed paper. Gently tap these seams instead with a smoothing brush.

Things you should know

Keep changing the blades in your knife to ensure a clean trim line. Use a knife with snap-away blades for convenience.

Good tip

Clean the paste from your scissors every time you use them. This ensures cleaner work and a cleaner cut.

A Press against the top of the wall

B Wipe away excess paste

C Smooth the joins with a seam roller

HANGING PATTERNED WALLPAPER

Forward planning is essential when hanging patterned paper, and complete beginners will probably find it easiest to stick to a small 'all over' pattern which does not require matching and will also help to disguise mistakes. Leave the bold retro prints until you have gained a little experience.

Buying patterned paper

Matching different types of paper results in varying amounts of waste. Take this into account when estimating how much you need to buy.

How much of any pattern you will see depends on the pattern repeat measurement. Vertical patterns repeat anywhere from 25–635 mm (1–25 in). The greater the distance between repeats, the more paper you will need for matching, the more rolls you will need to buy, and the more waste you will create.

Check the label for additional advice.

Pattern types

Free match: This is a continuous pattern which doesn't need matching, hang the same way you would hang plain or woodchip paper.

Straight match: This paper has the same type of pattern running down both edges of the paper, and the pattern continues directly across the strips. The same part of the pattern is always the same distance from the ceiling in every strip. You will need to ensure there

is enough overlap at the top and bottom of each piece to exactly align the motifs and allow for trimming.

Offset or drop match: This pattern runs diagonally across the wall, and the pattern in every other strip is the same at the ceiling line. The edges of this paper will be different on each side, with motifs staggered between the drops. You will need to allow extra paper for matching – the pattern repeat length will be shown on the label. The design may form a diamond grid effect and generally the larger the pattern, the larger the drop.

Random or plain match: Read the label carefully to determine how this type of pattern should be hung, as it will vary from design to design. For example, a textured match will look better if each length is hung the opposite way up. This will help to keep the pattern random.

▶ **above right** Small prints work well in smaller spaces and will result in less paper wastage

Free match

Straight match

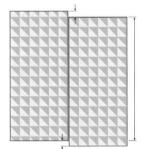

Offset match

Random match

Finding your starting point

1 When working with large or bold patterns, it's best to start papering from the room's focal point. This may be a feature such as chimney breast or the centre of the first wall you see on entering the room (**diagram A**).

2 The pattern will need to look balanced and so will need to be hung symmetrically. Use a measuring tape to find the centre point of the wall or feature you are starting from, and draw a plumb line there. Now you have a choice to make. Do you want to centre your first strip of paper on this line, or hang a strip of paper either side of the line? Your decision will depend on the pattern you are working with – which method looks best? Remember your decision will also have an effect on the other drops of paper around the room, the best choice may give you a less awkward cut at another point.

3 If you are hanging an all-over pattern, start at a window. Work away from the window in both directions towards the darkest corner of the room (**diagram B**). If you have two adjacent windows on a wall, centre the paper between them.

A Starting at the chimney breast

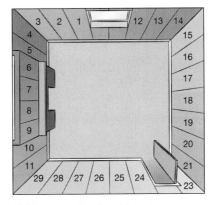

B The correct order of hanging

Cutting

1 Unroll the paper, pattern side up. Measure the full length of the drop, allowing 100 mm (4 in) extra. Before cutting the first strip, hold the wallpaper against the wall to find the best breaking point in the pattern – this is the point where you want the pattern to meet the ceiling line.

2 Double check the length before cutting additional pieces from several rolls at once. Ensure the pattern matches the first piece on several lengths. This reduces interruptions later on and helps you to match patterns more easily.

3 Mark the top of each piece on the back of the work to remind you which way to hang it. Use bulldog clips to clamp the pieces together and stop them rolling up (**diagram A**).

4 Mark cutting lengths of paper from the roll. You may have to allow extra for matching the pattern on adjacent strips – check before cutting. As a rule, you can usually cut four pieces of paper per roll. But if the pattern is very big, you may only get three or even two pieces per roll.

▲ **above** Match the pattern carefully as you work around the room and mark a new plumb line after turning a corner

Good tip

Depending on the paper's pattern, you might find that cutting strips from alternate rolls of paper saves wastage.

Good tip

Save remnants left over after pattern matching strips, they are often useful for small areas such as above windows and doors.

Hanging

1 Match the pattern carefully as you hang each strip, making sure the edges butt up snugly. It is best to match the pattern first at eye level so that any mismatches in a long strip will occur at the top and bottom and won't be quite so noticeable.

2 Remember to mark a new plumb line every time you turn a corner. This is essential to keep your pattern from gradually sliding 'downhill'.

Mismatches

There is generally a point in the room where you won't be able to match the pattern between two strips. Plan ahead so that the mismatch occurs in the least visible corner of the room, or over the door or window.

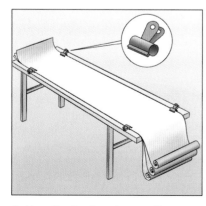

A Use clips to stop pieces rolling up

HANGING OTHER WALLCOVERINGS

Lose the conventional notions! Wallpapering isn't all about unrolling, cutting and pasting in the old fashioned way – as technology has moved on, so too have wallpapers. There are lots of great new choices available, so whether you are looking for a way to save time – with a pre-pasted or paste the wall option – or want to find that wow factor to really make a design statement – you'll definitely find an option to suit you.

Pre-pasted papers

Pre-pasted papers are pretty much what they say they are – they do not need pasting in the conventional way. Instead the paper should be immersed in water to activate the paste already applied to the back. There are a number of ways of doing this – full instructions will be supplied with the paper and these should be carefull followed. The majority of pre-pasted papers are vinyls, and good for a beginner as there is no messy pasting to contend with.

Handy Hint

The soaking needed to activate the paste can stretch the paper a little so make sure each piece is closely fitted to the next to prevent gaps arising.

Paste the wall

Some papers require the wall to be pasted rather than the paper – in this case, follow the instructions given by the manufacturer. This type of paper may appeal to beginners who are not confident about the pasting process, however take care when attaching the paper to the wall so it doesn't catch and tear.

Handy Hint

Apply the adhesive to a wider area than the paper's width. Then you won't have to apply the paste for the next strip right up to the edge of the paper. Use a roller to apply adhesive easily.

Self-adhesive paper

This requires no pasting or soaking – simply peel off the backing and stick the paper in place. It is commonly used for paper borders.

Handy Hint

Use a horizontal guideline to ensure self-adhesive borders are lined up correctly.

Woodchip

Made from two layers of paper bonded with a sprinkling of wood chips between them. Designed to be painted, it is easy to hang as it does not need matching. Hang as for standard paper.

Handy Hint

Some surfaces feel abrasive to the touch and so are not suitable for use in areas where they are likely to be rubbed up against such as narrow hallways or stairways, or children's rooms.

Strippable and peelable

These papers, as the names suggest, are easier to remove for redecoration than standard wall coverings. Strippable options pull off the wall in one piece, while peelable papers usually come off in a couple of layers.

▼ **below** Digital wallpaper is not for the faint-hearted: here the bar area in a restaurant is given a contemporary makeover with a striking digital print

Handy Hint

Strippable papers are ideal if you like to decorate every few years and don't want to spend lots of time stripping walls. They are also perfect for awkward-to-reach spaces such as a high stairwell.

Digital wallpaper

A relatively new addition to the wallpaper family, digital technology allows you to create your own individual statement and is ideal for a dramatic impact feature wall. Companies offering this service generally have a large photo library from which you can choose the image you wish to have transferred to paper – alternatively use a personal photo for a really unique appeal.

PAPERING CEILINGS

A papered ceiling adds a touch of luxury and warmth to a room and is a clever way of hiding surface imperfections in older properties. It is a job that is best undertaken with two people – particularly if you've never papered a ceiling before.

Safety first

It is advisable to build some type of platform to work from, both for safety and comfort. It is possible to hire trestles and scaffold boards for this purpose – scaffold boards come in various lengths to suit any size of room. Make sure this is very firmly fixed before you begin.

Calculating how many rolls

Measure ceiling length and width and multiply to get the total area to be covered.

L x W = Total area

Check the wallpaper label to find the area covered by one roll. Then divide this into the total area to be covered to get the number of rolls needed. Remember to add extra for wastage and pattern matching.

Total area to be covered
───────────── = **Number of rolls needed, plus one for wastage**
Area covered by one roll

Getting started

1 First erect a working platform using the trestles and scaffold boards. Set the height so you don't have to bend or stretch too far while working. Ideally you should be able to touch the ceiling from the scaffold with the palm of your hand.

2 Take down lampshades and light fittings. Remove all old paper and any loose paint and plaster, and fill cracks. If gloss painted, rub with 40-grit abrasive paper wrapped around a cork block or use a sanding block. Wash thoroughly with sugar soap to remove all traces of dirt.

3 Prepare paste, according to manufacturer's instructions.

Finding your starting point

1 It is generally advisable to hang patterned paper parallel to the main window, working away from the window towards the other end of the room to minimize shadows made by the joins (**diagram A**).

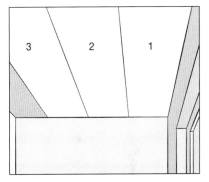

A Work away from the window

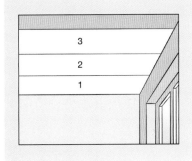

Marking a guideline

1 Measure the width of the paper and deduct 25 mm (1 in). Working at the short end of the ceiling, measure this distance from the corner along the longer wall and mark with a pencil. Moving along the short end of the ceiling, measure this distance from the opposite corner and mark. Use a chalk line to connect these two points along the ceiling. This will be your starting line (**diagram A**).

Cutting

1 Measure and cut your first length of paper, adding on an extra 100 mm (4 in) for trimming. You can now either cut all the remaining lengths you will need – to save interruptions as you work – or cut as you go. Mark each length at the top to remind you

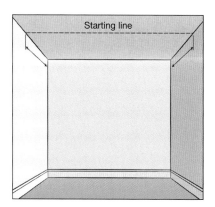

A Marking a guideline

which way to hang it. If cutting several pieces together, clamp them with bulldog clips to stop them rolling up.

Pasting

1 Paste the paper, working out towards the edge. Fold over 30–40 cm (12–16 in), pasted sides touching, and continue until you have a loose concertina. Don't flatten the ends of the folds. Leave to soak if required by the manufacturer (**diagram B**).

Hanging

1 Stand side on to the chalk line, facing the side wall. Pull the top fold of the concertina open and position it on the ceiling against the chalk line. Allow an overlap on the end wall of about 50 mm (2 in) (**diagram C**).

2 Use the brush to smooth down the centre section and out to each edge, making sure there are no air bubbles, and that the paper follows the line.

3 Release the next fold and smooth out with the brush as before. Walk along the scaffold, slowly releasing the paper and brushing it out as you go.

4 Trim the edges by smoothing paper into the angles and cutting with a wallpaper scissors. If you are hanging paper on the walls, leave a surplus of about 10 mm (½ in) at each end to hide any gaps when you paper the walls. If papering up to coving, crease the paper into the corner and cut off the excess using a broad knife.

5 Hang the next strip of paper, butting up tightly to the first. Continue to cover the rest of the ceiling. The last piece will inevitably be narrower than a normal width. Measure the gap, add on 50 mm (2 in) and cut a length to this size. Paste, fold, hang and trim as usual.

Rolling joins

1 When the paper is nearly dry, smooth the joins with a seam roller. If the paper is embossed, use the corner of a felt roller.

Good tip

If working with two people, one can hold and align the paper while the other smoothes it onto the ceiling.

B Fold the paper

C Position on the ceiling

▲ **above** Cosy up a large room by papering the ceiling as well as the walls

Good tip

Minimize the work involved in papering a ceiling by choosing a paper with a small repeating pattern that is easily matched.

Good idea

Paste the paper and book it as normal (see page 38), then wrap it around a broom handle to unroll onto the ceiling for easier hanging.

Sloping ceilings and dormer windows

Papering a sloping ceiling and around a dormer window calls for a slightly different approach than papering flat surfaces or around a standard window. However it is a skill that is increasingly useful as more and more of us convert the spaces in lofts and under the stairs into bedrooms and cloakrooms.

Dormer windows

The most important thing to get right when papering around this type of window is the order of hanging the strips. The correct order of work is shown here (**diagram A**). Paper the section of flat wall directly under the window first, next paper the sides of the window, finally paper the sloping ceiling section and underneath walls.

▲ **above** Choose a free match paper when tackling awkward areas such as a sloping ceiling

Sloping ceilings

While the basic principle is the same as for papering walls, you may find easier to use 'paste the wall' paper, rather than standard wallpaper. Pasting the wall gives a 'tacky' surface to which the paper will adhere to more easily.

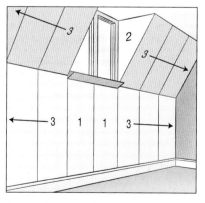

A Papering around dormer windows

Handy Hints

- When papering an attic bedroom or under-stairs cloakroom with sloping ceilings, choose a paper that doesn't have to be matched, such as a random floral.
- There will be a mis-match of pattern between the sides of the dormer window and the sloping ceiling – this can be disguised by using a border, alternatively you could paint the sides of the window to create a contrast.
- Alternatively use two contrasting papers to tidy up uneven joins between the sloping and flat parts of the ceiling, or use a border to disguise the join if using the same paper.

TROUBLESHOOTING

Despite your best efforts, you may still find you are left with a few awkward problems once the job is finished. But don't panic, all is not lost. Learn the secrets of the professionals to iron out any sticky areas.

Peeling paper

If the paper starts to lift slightly it means you did not paste each strip right to the edge – take care when pasting and get this right. There is a special brush you can purchase afterwards that allows you to apply paste to the edges easily. If the paper is peeling off, it suggests you did not apply the paste evenly; in extreme cases you may need to re-paste and re-hang. However, it might also mean you did not prepare the surface properly.

Air bubbles on surface

If air bubbles linger on the surface of the paper after it has dried, make a neat incision in the bubble using a craft knife (**diagram A**) and lift the edges gently. Apply paste and smooth back into place with a seam roller.

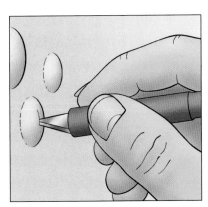

A Make a neat incision in the bubble

Paste bubbles

If paste is applied too thickly, it will result in unsightly bumps when the paper is hung. To rectify, make a tiny pinprick in the centre of the bump and gently squeeze out the excess paste before wiping clean.

Uneven ceiling line

Disguise a less-than-perfect line at the ceiling by pasting a narrow, patterned border along the top of the wall.

Uneven or bumpy surface finish

Problems will arise if you do not prepare and clean the surface adequately before hanging paper. It is vital to remove any loose paint and plaster from the wall and fill in any holes with a fine surface filler, sanding smooth afterwards. Wash walls thoroughly with sugar soap to remove all traces of dirt and grease. If surfaces are beyond repair, consider hanging papers designed to hide imperfections, such as heavy grade lining paper, sturdy woodchip or embossed designs.

Paper shrinkage

Heavy and embossed papers may shrink slightly once hung if the paste is not left to soak on each strip before hanging – check the instructions carefully. Some specialist papers need to be hung as overlapped strips to allow for shrinkage – these are best left to professional decorators.

Other problems to avoid

Mismatched paper

Marking the top of the paper on the reverse with a pencil before pasting will ensure you position it correctly when you take it to the wall for hanging.

Hanging paper upside down

Don't assume a paper comes off the roll in the direction it will be hung. Check the design to ensure you are hanging it the right way up.

Smeared or dirty paper and woodwork

Clean excess paste off the surface of the paper and woodwork with a sponge or damp cloth as you work, otherwise it will result in smears. Keep tools and hands clean also to avoid marking the paper.

Tears or jagged edges

Always use high quality tools in tiptop condition; make sure your broad blade knife and scissors are sharp enough to trim edges neatly.

Uneven joins and crooked pattern

Always use a plumb line to position your first strip of paper accurately and ensure the adjoining strips are hung straight. Mark a new plumb line each time you turn a corner, to stop your pattern 'falling over'.

wallpaper projects

The projects that follow show you how to deal with all the situations and problems you will come across when wallpapering a room. From dealing with obstacles such as light switches and radiators, to papering round windows and doors and dealing wtih alcoves and archways, all the information you need is given, step by step

Once you have mastered the skills, it's time to get creative! Find out how to combine two or more papers in one room, how to create a stunning feature wall, make the most of architectural features such as dado rails or panels and how to use borders to best effect – as well as lots of style tips on working with different 'looks' from stripes to stickers to framing tricks.

PAPERING AROUND CORNERS

So you've mastered papering in a straight line and completed a full wall. Now comes the corner! It's probably the first maneouvre you will have to tackle when papering a full room – this step-by-step guide outlines the tricks of the trade to take you through it successfully.

◀ **left** Use a plumb line to keep
edges straight when papering around
corners

◀ **far left** Extra care should be
taken with a geometric pattern such as
a stripe when working round corners

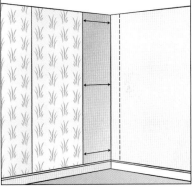

A Measure the distance to the corner

B Press the paper into the corner

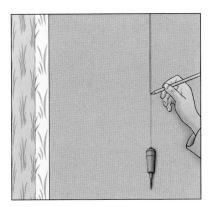

C Mark a new plumb line

Internal corners

1 Measure the distance from the strip of paper on the wall to the corner – take the measurement in a few different places along the length of the paper for accuracy. If different – a frequent occurance as walls are often not purely vertical or 'true plumb' – use the longest measurement. Any slight break in the pattern will be negligible, particularly as it is in a corner (**diagram A**). Cut the next strip 25 mm (1 in) wider than this measurement using a sharp knife and a straight edge.

2 Line up the new strip alongside the last one you hung and press into the corner carefully (**diagram B**). Use a seam roller to secure it safely and firmly along the edge.

3 Before you continue along the new wall, mark a plumb line, a distance that is 25 mm (1 in) less than one roll's width, from the corner (**diagram C**). Lay the next sheet of paper along this line, tapping it carefully into the corner over the existing strip. Again, use a seam roller to secure it firmly over the overlap.

4 Use a sharp knife to cut through the overlapping pieces of paper, about 5 mm (¼ in) from the corner and at the seam of the overlap.

5 Remove the outer piece of overlapping paper, then lift up the outer paper enough to get at the paper underneath. Remove this along the cut and lay the outer piece back onto the wall.

6 Use the seam roller to smooth back firmly into place.

External corners

1 As with internal corners measure the distance from the strip of paper on the wall to the corner – taking the measurement in several places for accuracy – and cut the next strip 25 mm (1 in) wider to bend around the corner (**diagram A**). If the measurement is within 120 mm (6 in) of a full sheet, use a full sheet, cutting a diagonal slit at the top so it will bend neatly around the corner. Paste and hang this strip.

2 Mark a plumb line on the new wall, a roll's width away from the corner. Hang the next sheet of wallpaper from the corner to the plumb line, overlapping the previous sheet where it bends around the corner (**diagram B**).

3 Use a sharp knife to cut through the overlapping pieces of paper, about 5 mm (¼ in) from the corner and the seam of the overlap, and peel away the excess (**diagram C**).

Things you should know

Papering around corners is not difficult in itself. So why should you give it special attention? The difficulty lies in the fact that corners are rarely vertical or 'true plumb'. However your paper must be! This is why it is extremely important to follow the steps outlined.

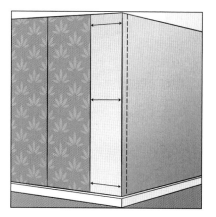

A Measure into the corner

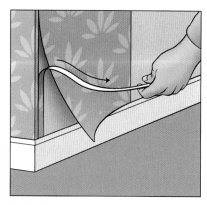

B Hang the next sheet

C Peel away the excess paper

Be careful!

Don't try to work around a corner in one piece. Quite often corners are not square and the edge of the paper will move out of line. Bubbles and creases may also develop.

Take note

Mark a new plumb line every time you turn a corner. This is essential with patterned paper to keep your pattern from gradually sliding "downhill".

Good tip

An inconspicuous corner is often a good place from where to start wallpapering. To fit your first sheet correctly, measure the width of your strip of wallpaper. Subtract 25 mm (1 in) for overlap and mark a line on the wall this distance from the corner. Use a plumb to ensure your line is perfectly vertical. Now use this as your guideline to hang the first strip of paper.

▶ **right** Papering around corners is not difficult once you follow the correct procedure

PAPERING AROUND WINDOWS AND DOORS

You may encounter a room without windows if papering a small downstairs cloakroom – or maybe even a room without conventional doors if papering a loft accessed by a trapdoor. However you are highly unlikely to find a room that has neither! Papering around windows and doors requires specific know-how to achieve a professional finish. Our step-by-step guide shows you how.

▶ **right** Remove any nearby obstacles, such as wall hooks, to make working around a door frame easier

◀ **left** Use a straight edge when cutting paper around a window opening for a professional finish

Doorways

1 When you come to a doorway, hang the next strip of wallpaper as normal, butting it up to the previous strip and allowing the edge to overlap the doorframe.

2 Make a diagonal cut in the waste paper towards the corner of the doorframe (**diagram A**). Brush the paper firmly into place against the side of the frame, and use the brush to crease along the frame's edge. Trim off the waste.

3 Brush the paper above the door into place and trim off the waste, leaving a 12 mm (½ in) overlap pasted to the top of the frame (**diagram B**).

4 Cut and hang the next piece as normal to fill the space over the door. Repeat the steps above when you reach the other side of the frame.

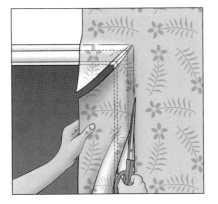

A Make a diagonal cut

B Brush the paper above the door

Windows

1 As with papering around a doorway, when you come to a window frame that is flush to the wall, hang the next strip of paper as normal, butting it up to the previous strip and allowing the edge to overlap the frame.

2 Make a diagonal cut in the waste paper towards the corner of the frame. Brush the paper firmly into place against the side of the frame, use the scissors to crease along the edge of the frame and trim off the waste.

3 To cut around the windowsill, first make a horizontal cut up to the top corner of the sill. Then make a diagonal cut into the bottom corner of the sill (**diagram A**). Feel for the end of the sill and make a series of cuts up to this line.

4 Use the brush to force the paper into the angles made by the wall, the frame and the window sill. Mark and trim the waste.

A Cut into the corner of the sill

▲ **above** Draw attention to an attractive feature such as these French-style shuttered windows by using a contrasting paper on the supporting wall

Window and door reveals

1 Cut a width of paper equal to the depth of the horizontal reveal plus 50 mm (2 in) (**diagram A**). Paste and fold the piece, but don't hang it yet.

2 Paste a length of covering and butt it up against the last piece of paper you hung before the reveal. Mark with a pencil the width of this piece on the edge of the horizontal reveal. Then put the piece to one side.

3 Take the original piece and fix it to the reveal, lining it up with the pencil mark. Smooth it onto the reveal and make a cut through the overlap at the corner.

4 Carefully tear 25 mm (1 in) off the overlap and flatten it round the corners with a brush. The torn edge, when covered, will show less obviously than a straight cut line (**diagram B**).

5 Hang the full-length piece. Make a horizontal cut with the scissors where the piece hangs over the opening. Fold the overlap into the reveal up to the frame (**diagram C**). Crease and remove the waste.

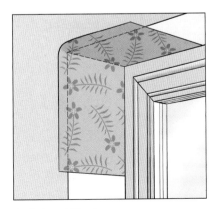

A Cut a width of paper

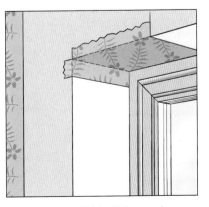

B Tear 25 mm (1 in) off the overlap

C Fold the overlap into the reveal

PAPERING AROUND OBSTACLES

Standard obstacles you will almost always encounter when papering a room are light switches, electric sockets and radiators. You may also have to deal with wall lights, fireplaces, and, if papering a ceiling, centre plates or ceiling roses. Papering a stairway involves working around one of the biggest obstacles you will ever encounter – a staircase! But it's not difficult when you know how, and it won't take long to master the correct techniques.

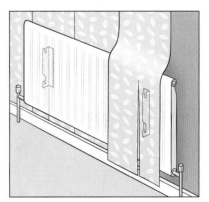

53

PAPERING AROUND OBSTACLES

Remember ...

It is usually best to remove obstacles when papering, however this is not always possible. Follow the guidelines below to learn how to deal with every possible obstacle you might encounter, and avoid ruining an otherwise perfect job.

Light switches and electric sockets

1 For safety, first turn off the electricity for that circuit at the mains. Unscrew the faceplate from the wall, remove any old wallcovering from underneath and replace.

2 Hang wallpaper lightly over the fitting, as you normally would, and once the paper is in place make diagonal cuts from the centre of the plate to its corners (**diagram A**). Trim the waste, leaving approx 12 mm (½ in) all around (**diagram B**). Smooth paper into position along the wall.

3 Loosen the screws holding the plate in place and use a brush to tap the surplus paper under the plate (**diagram C**). Tighten the screws. Wait until the adhesive is dry before you turn the electricity back on.

▲ **above** Papering neatly round light switches gives a professional finish

◀ **left** Take extra care when papering a stairwell – build a safe work platform to make the job easier

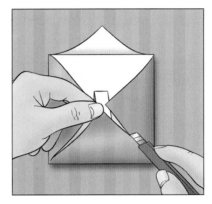

A Make diagonal cuts

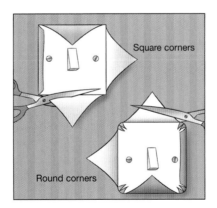

Square corners

Round corners

B Trim the waste

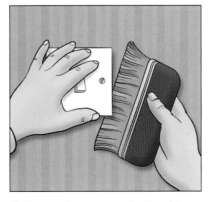

C Tap surplus paper under the plate

Radiators

1 It is best to remove radiators and paper the wall as normal, replacing them afterwards. Drain the radiator first.

2 If this is not possible, paste the strip of wallpaper as normal and attach to the wall above the radiator. To paper around the brackets, slit paper from the bottom edge at the appropriate point, and smooth down either side of the radiator's fixing brackets (**diagram D**).

3 Alternatively, measure the position of the brackets and transfer these measurements to the length of paper. Slit the paper along the marked line before hanging.

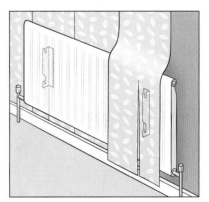

D Slit the paper from the bottom up

Light plates

1 You may encounter circular light plates when papering either walls or ceilings; these are reasonably easy to navigate around but remember to turn off the electricity for that circuit at the mains as you would for light switches and sockets.

2 Hang the paper lightly over the obstacle. Mark the centre and make a series of cuts from the centre to the edges. Push the paper back into place. Mark where the paper meets the edge of the plate and trim neatly (**diagram A**).

Ceiling rose

Turn off electricity for that particular circuit at the mains. Hang paper loosely over the ceiling rose. Then if the rose is:

Near the edge of the paper
Cut from the edge of the paper to the centre of the ceiling rose. Make a series of cuts from the centre to the edge of the rose. Brush the paper over and around the rose. Allow to dry, then trim with a sharp knife.

In the middle of the paper
Feel for the centre of the rose and make a hole in the paper. Feed the light flex and bulb holder through the hole, and brush the paper around. Trim the paper, making a series of cuts from the paper at the edge of the rose to the centre, when dry (**diagram B**).

Fireplaces

1 Papering around a fireplace is similar to papering around a door or a window. Take plenty of time and extra care here, as there are usually lots of tricky angles to negotiate.

2 Hang the paper lightly, allowing it to overlap the fireplace. Mark your cutting line with scissors and then make careful cuts in the waste paper. Ease the paper back into place around the edge of the fireplace and then continue to make cuts down the side of the fireplace, easing the paper into place as you go (**diagrams C, D and E**).

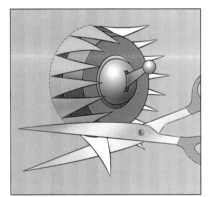

A Trim away the excess

B Trim away the excess paper

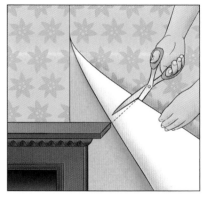

D Make careful cuts

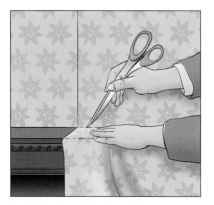

C Mark the cutting line with scissors

E Ease the paper into place

Stairway

1 The main problems when papering a stairwell are the extra long drops on the side walls and the uneven 'floor' – the stairs! For these reasons, it is best to build a safe work platform over the stairs, and to work with a second person.

2 Start by hanging the longest drop, remembering to plumb the wall first and to allow enough length to trim at the angled skirting board. Apply plenty of paste to each strip so it doesn't dry out as you work it into place down the long wall. Fold each piece concertina style to make it easy to carry, and use your helper to support the weight of the pasted length while you apply it.

3 Work away from the first strip in each direction, and paper the head wall above the stairs last (**diagram A**).

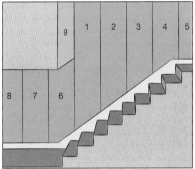

A Work away from the first strip

Good idea

If a length needs a lot of trimming the edges may begin to dry out and start to peel off the wall before you can brush the entire strip into place. As a quick fix measure to prevent this happening, keep a paintbrush and a mug of paste handy to brush extra paste onto the paper seam wherever it's needed.

Good tip

Use the back of a pair of scissors or bristle brush to mark the cutting line rather than a pencil which might leave marks.

▲ **above** Treat an obstacle like an alcove in the same way as you would a door frame

PAPERING AN ARCH

When tackling a room with an archway, some careful planning is called for before you start papering. There are a number of ways to approach it, and your final decision will depend on the shape of the arch, the type of paper being used, pattern size and personal preference. Think carefully before you start work – an arch is an attractive feature in a room that will be spoiled if not papered correctly.

◀ **left** Papering an arch is particularly effective when you want to create a flow between two rooms

Remember ...

Arches are best papered with a plain or random-patterned paper, as pattern-matching is difficult between the curved and flat surfaces. If you have your heart set on a complicated pattern, perhaps consider using a contrasting plain paper on the archway to make it a feature wall.

Rectangular arch

1 Before you start papering, plan the layout of the wall containing the arch so that the first strip will overlap the arch to cover it (this is most easily done by planning where the arch strips will fall, then measuring backwards to your starting corner) (**diagram A**).

2 The first strip should be aligned so that enough of the right hand side overlaps the arch to cover it. Make a horizontal cut precisely at the top edge of the arch. Fit the paper around the left-hand vertical side of the arch.

3 Next cut the header strips over the archway long enough to cover the underside of the arch, and hang as normal.

4 Hang the final strip at the side in the same way as the first strip was hung.

5 Finally, fill in the gaps on the undersides of the arch on the left and right hand sides by cutting matching pieces to fit. Tuck the top ends under the wallcovering on the face of the arch where the horizontal cuts were made and smooth the piece onto the underside of the arch to fill the space.

Curved arch

1 It is a good idea when papering a room with a curved arch, to start papering from the arch. Measure the arch to find the centre point, hang a plumb line and mark a vertical line for your starting point. Depending on the size of the arch, either centre your first piece of paper over this line, or hang a strip of paper either side of the line so the join is centred over the arch.

2 Hang the strips as normal, trimming away the excess to leave 25 mm (1 in) for the overlap.

3 Make narrow 'V' cuts at 300 mm (12 in) intervals at the curved points and fold the waste into place under the top of the arch and down each side (**diagram B**). When both sides of the arch are covered, cut strips of paper – pattern matching from the bottom up – paste and hang on the underside of the arch (**diagram C**).

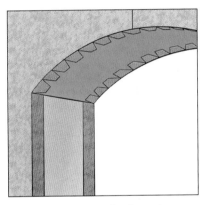

A Plan the layout of the wall

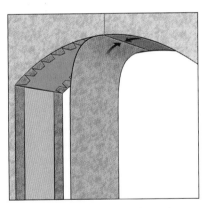

B Fold the waste under the arch

C Paper the underside of the arch

Good tip

If you are not papering the wall on the other side of the archway, don't cut the paper right to the edge – instead leave a tiny gap of about 7 mm (¼ in) to the edge of the arch to prevent fraying.

Handy hint

For a neat finish, trim the inside strips exactly to the wall thickness.

USING BORDERS

Borders give your wallpaper a neat finishing touch, whether used at ceiling, picture rail or dado height, and are also a great way to link contrasting design schemes within a room or run of rooms. But there's a lot more to borders than this – used creatively they can make their own design statement. Follow our guide to hanging borders, as well as hints and tips for alternative ways to use them, and make a really individual statement in your home.

Hanging a wallpaper border

A border adds impact to a wallpaper scheme when used at ceiling or picture rail height, and breaks up a large expanse of wall when used at dado height. If wallpapering half way up or down a wall, a border is essential to provide a neat trim. Use paint or a contrasting paper to complete the rest of the wall.

1 Decide the position of your border and draw light pencil guidelines all around the room, marking either the top or bottom guiding line. Use a spirit level and steel ruler to mark accurately. This is not necessary if hanging a border at the top of the wall – just use the edge of the ceiling as a guide.

2 Borders are supplied in long lengths and look best hung in a straight run across a wall with overlapping seams at the corners. Cut lengths to match the wall dimensions, allow 50 mm (2 in) at the ends for trimming. Remember to pattern match if necessary.

3 If it requires pasting, mix paste according to manufacturer's instructions, then fold concertina style, lapping the pasted sides together as when booking standard wallcoverings (**diagram A**). Position one end of the border in a corner, using the pencil guideline to keep it straight, then unroll along the wall, brushing into place as you go

◄ **left** Vertical borders create an eye-catching feature wall

Good tip

To make a high ceiling seem lower for a more intimate feel in a room, paint the area above a picture rail border with the same shade as used on the ceiling.

(**diagram B**). If using a self adhesive border, peel off a short length of the backing paper to start, then continue to peel a little at a time as you fix it along the wall.

4 Cut the next strip to match the pattern on the previous strip, allowing for a little overlap. Butt join the lengths of border by sticking the start of the second length over the end of the first one. Double cut the overlap carefully using your steel ruler and a sharp knife (**diagram C**). Remove the excess from the top length and open up the joint to remove excess from the first length. Smooth the ends back into place using your wallpaper brush. Use a seam roller to secure the joins (**diagram D**).

5 To finish, make an unobtrusive butt joint by cutting through both layers where they overlap, close to the corner on the first wall and removing the excess as above.

A Paste and fold the border

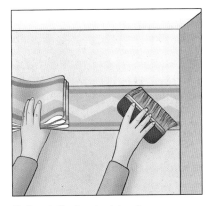

B Brush the border into place

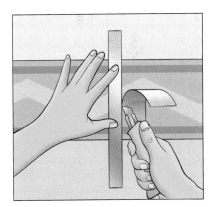

C Cut away the overlap

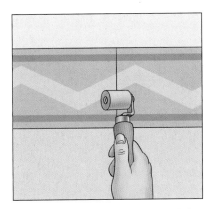

D Use a seam roller to secure the joins

Designer tips

- Hang borders vertically to create stripes and give a room a designer look. This will also have the effect of making a low ceiling seem higher, creating a spacious feeling in smaller rooms. This look works on both painted and papered walls, but choose patterns and colours carefully to coordinate.
- Borders are a great way of giving a room a cohesive feel, tying together different effects such as painted and papered walls. Using both paint and paper in one room can look very stylish but there is also a danger it may make a room feel fragmented. A border gives a unified look, and is a great way of linking different areas of a room that may be decorated separately, such as a bedroom and dressing room or en suite bathroom. It can also link a group of rooms such as hallway and living areas that are decorated differently but complement each other.

- For an alternative look, use a narrow border on wallpapered walls and a wider complementary border on a painted feature wall to create interest for the eye.
- Using a border along the baseboards will draw attention downwards to highlight a beautiful wood floor. Or fit a border along the risers of steps and stairs for an eye-catching effect.
- An extra wide or oversize border hung between picture and dado rail height creates an eye-catching feature in a room and is a very contemporary use of the traditional border strip.
- Tie your design scheme neatly together using sections of your chosen wallpaper border as trimming along the edges of shelves and bookcases.

Good idea

If unsure what height to hang your border, hang with poster putty or low-tack masking tape first to try out different effects.

Handy hint

If using a border to create a dado rail, a trompe l'oeil border that looks like decorative wooden moulding is a great option. Use a double strip for even more impact.

Remember ...

If the border needs pasting, make sure you buy the correct paste to suit both your border and the wall surface. If sticking it to emulsion or ordinary wallpaper, standard paste is fine, however if working with a washable or vinyl surface you will need to buy special ready-mixed border adhesive.

▶ **right** Give a room the perfect finishing touch with a wide textured border at picture rail height

USING STRIPES

Whether you want to evoke the classic look of Regency style in a period home, add a touch of texture to a dado or feature wall or simply make a bold statement in a dining room, lounge or hallway, stripes are the perfect answer. Popular for centuries, from ancient times right up to the present, stripes can be used in a variety of ways to create an array of different looks. It's all down to the way you use them. Be as bold – or subtle – as you like.

▲ **above** Horizontal stripes draw the eye out and make narrow spaces seem wider

◀ **left** Play with pattern and mix stripes with florals; choose complementary colours to make the look work

Hanging stripes

1 Relax – it's not as difficult as it might first appear. It is vital to hang the first strip absolutely vertical of course, otherwise the pattern will start to lean as you work around the wall, and leaning stripes will not enhance your design scheme in any way!

2 Use a plumb line to mark your starting point, and keep a check with a spirit level as you work to ensure the stripes line up accurately all the way around. Mark a new plumb line each time you turn a corner and start papering on a new wall.

3 Stripes are classified as a 'free match' paper, which means the pattern is continuous and does not need matching, so you can just cut the drops according to the length you need them. However, it is essential that you hang the paper the right way around each time – ie not upside down – so that the pattern follows the correct layout of stripe 1/ stripe 2 all the way around the room.

Looks with stripes

From the period of Louis XVI to the English Regency era of the 1800s, from Art Deco glamour to the boldness of the 1970s, stripes have continually resurrected themselves and taken their place in great design schemes over the centuries. They have also existed far from formal dining rooms and glamorous living rooms in the weaving and pottery work of native people from Mexico to Africa and beyond.

But why do stripes remain so popular in contemporary design schemes? One reason is the feeling of symmetry and balance they bring to a room, another is the fact they mix very well with other patterns such as florals and checks or can be used solely on their own to add texture to a flat space.

There are a number of looks to be achieved with stripes. Most obvious are those detailed above – a great way to bring the period feel of Regency or French aristocracy to a room, re-create the glamour of the Art Deco '20s and '30s or the retro style of the '70s. Or choose narrow stripes and pinstripes for a country cottage feel.

If you are drawn to using stripes but are not feeling confident about using them all around a room, use striped wallpaper to make an impact beneath a dado rail and paint or paper the wall above in a complementary shade and style.

If you want to add more texture to your scheme, why not mix your patterns and use a pretty floral paper underneath a dado, with stripes above. The key is to keep patterns in scale and use common colours to tie the look together.

If you feel the room is too small and will be overpowered by an all-over pattern of stripes, opt for a striped feature wall instead.

Tricks with stripes

- Vertical stripes will visually emphasize a room's height and are ideal for rooms that appear a bit cramped as the stripes will distract the eye from limited floor space. This is the reason that stripes are frequently used in entrance hallways.

- Used in the opposite way – hung horizontally – stripes will draw the eye out and make narrow rooms appear wider. Horizontal stripes will also have the visual effect of lowering a room with a high ceiling and make it feel more cosy and intimate. This look really suits a contemporary space, but will only work with wide stripes.

▲ **above** The stripes in this wallpaper are echoed in the texture and pattern of the soft furnishings

◀ **left** Bold stripes make a dramatic statement when combined with a traditional flock paper

Design trick

Leave a border of about 500 mm (20 in) all around the edge of the wall to create an attractive panelled effect with your striped wallpaper.

Handy hint

Choose the width of your stripes carefully. Large stripes in a small room will overpower the space, narrow stripes in a large room will appear to blend together and the effect will be lost.

PAINTING PAPER

Drawn to the warm look of wallpaper but also like the freshness of paint? Cursed with cracked walls or bumpy surfaces that are a decorator's nightmare? If your answer is yes to either question – or in fact both – you need a combination approach, wallpaper you can paint over! With a good selection of options on offer, from easy-to-hang woodchip to luxurious Anaglypta, you will find something to suit your taste, budget and even your problem walls.

Remember ...

Hang your paper and let it dry overnight before painting the next day. Ensure you apply the correct paint to your chosen paper – check manufacturer's instructions for advice.

Be careful

Use a roller to paint your paper rather than a brush – you'll get better coverage and it's faster. If hanging specialist embossed papers such as Lincrusta and Anaglypta, it is essential to purchase the correct type of roller that will not flatten the raised pattern and damage it.

◀ **left** Paint over specialist paper for a dramatic effect in a bathroom

▼ **below** Invest in the correct tools when painting Lincrusta to protect the pattern

Woodchip

The budget 'quick-fix' option for wallpaper you can paint over, woodchip paper is manufactured by bonding lots of tiny chips of wood onto standard paper and is available in various grades, from fine to coarse, depending on the size of the chips.

It is easy to hang, as it does not require matching, and can be used to achieve a variety of effects depending on the paint colour chosen. It is good for hiding surface imperfections in walls that are not suitable for painting directly onto the plaster, and will generally suit any surface.

▲ **above** Here embossed paper has been used as a border at ceiling height. For a dramatic effect, the textured pattern has been picked out in gold metallic paint

Textured and Embossed

Textured and embossed papers are available in a variety of effects, including wood, stone and brick, as well as more traditional designs. They are ideal for walls that are less than perfect, and can be painted after hanging – or at a later date to freshen up a tired scheme.

Papers crafted to imitate wooden panelling or stone or brickwork are much less expensive and easier to fit than the real thing. They are perfect for an all-over look, or to highlight a feature wall – they also look great at half height around a room to add definition to the space.

Lincrusta and Anaglypta

These richly textured papers are more expensive, heavier and harder to hang than the other options, but the finished effect is simply stunning and ideal for elegant living spaces. Patterns vary, from light patterns with a fine grain finish to heavily embossed designs that need to be carefully matched.

They require a slightly different hanging technique to standard papers, and in general are best left to professional decorators unless you are very confident of your wallpapering skills. Anaglypta should be pasted liberally with a heavy duty paste and left to soak for at least 10 minutes before hanging, while Lincrusta should be sponged with hot water until thoroughly soaked before pasting. Neither can be turned around corners – instead the edges should be cut to neatly butt up to the corner; fill any gaps at external corners with decorator's filler.

USING STICKERS

Let your imagination run wild! Stickers in every shape, size and colour imaginable are ideal for nurseries and children's room – and kids will love getting involved to help create their own design schemes. They are easy to apply and usually removable so when the theme dates or the children outgrow them, there's no difficulty redecorating. Suitable for use with painted or papered surfaces, the ideal way to keep the family entertained on a rainy afternoon.

A Start with a clean, dry surface

How to hang

There is a fantastic selection of themes and designs available, with something to suit every child, from the bookworm to the jungle lover.

1 For best effects, paint the wall first in one or more complementary shades of emulsion to give the perfect base for your artwork. Make sure your surface is flat, clean and dry (**picture A**).

2 Plot your wall plan on tracing paper before hanging stickers to help you create the best design.

3 Lay the sticker face down and pull the backing paper off part way (**picture B**).

4 Fold the liner back on itself and apply the exposed part of the sticker to the wall (**picture C**).

5 Slowly pull the backing off the remainder, smoothing the sticker to the wall with a brush or the palm of your hand as you do so.

6 Finish by softly rubbing over the surface of the sticker with a soft cloth or smoothing tool, taking care that the edges are securely attached (**picture D**). If using small stickers, remove all backing and apply straight to the wall.

◀ **left** Turn a child's room into a magical wonderland with easy-to-use stickers

B Pull the backing paper off part way

C Apply the exposed part to the wall

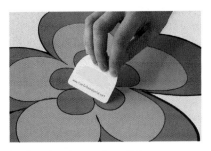

D Gently rub over the sticker

Remember ...

Stickers are not just for use on the wall, most are suitable for any smooth surfaces including metal, wood, glass, plastic and others, and so can be used to decorate doors, windows and furniture as well.

Be careful

Be careful not to bend the sticker when applying it to the wall, and ensure that the adhesive on the back does not come in contact with any other part of the sticker.

Remove backing slowly, as the sticker may stretch or tear if the backing is pulled off too quickly.

▶ **right** Plain walls can be transformed into galaxies with a little imagination and some clever designs

◀ **left** Use stickers to create fun features like a height chart in a bedroom

Troubleshooting

If you are left with unsightly air bubbles on the surface of your stickers after application, poke a pin through the bubble and press the air out.

The stickers may not adhere successfully to high gloss paint. If this is the case, it is possible to buy extra adhesion, follow the manufacturer's recommendations.

Remember ...

Most stickers on the market are removable and will not leave adhesive residue on the wall afterwards. They are usually printed on self-adhesive 'peel and stick' waterproof vinyl. They can be gently cleaned with a soft cloth or dampened paper towel, check the manufacturer's recommendations.

Safety first

For safety reasons do not place a sticker within reach of young children's cots or beds.

FRAMING WITH BORDERS

Borders are great for adding a finishing touch to a wallpapered room or providing a decorative trim for painted walls. But not only that! They can also be used to 'frame' a wall by creating panels that add texture and break up large expanses of plain paint or paper. Used with moulding, wallpaper border frames can create an eye-catching feature in a room. Get the look simply using standard borders or check out specialist manufacturers for a wider selection of effects.

◀ **left** Specialist border papers create architectural interest on an otherwise plain wall

◄ left Create stylish panels using variously sized border papers for added visual interest

How to create a border frame

1 Decide the position of your border and draw a guideline along the outer edge of the border on the wall with a pencil and steel ruler to help you position the paper accurately. Use a spirit level to ensure it is straight. Make sure the lines meet precisely at right angles.

2 Cut lengths to match the panel dimensions with an extra 50 mm (2 in) added at the end for trimming, allowing for pattern matching if necessary.

3 If the paper requires pasting, mix paste according to manufacturer's instructions, paste, then fold concertina style, lapping the pasted sides together.

4 Position one end of the border in a corner, using the pencil guideline to keep it straight, then unroll along the wall, brushing into place as you go. Wipe excess paste from the surface. If using a self adhesive border, peel off a short length of the backing paper to start, then continue to peel a little at a time as you fix it along the wall.

5 Stick the second strip over the end of the first one, keeping it straight along the pencil line. Repeat with the remaining strips to complete the panel.

6 To make a neat mitred corner joints where the borders form a frame, hold the steel ruler at 45 degrees across the corner and cut through both layers of paper with a sharp knife (**diagram A**).

Peel away the offcuts and smooth the border back into place using your wallpaper brush. Use a seam roller to smooth and secure joins.

7 Alternatively, stick corner medallions over the border strips to hide the seams and add extra architectural interest. Or make your own medallions using a design cut from the border.

A Creating a neat mitred corner

Looks with borders

- Border frames are an ideal way to add texture and architectural interest to a wall, whether painted or papered. Create a panelled effect with a series of borders, or just use one for a dramatic impact. The look works equally well on a plain door.
- Make a border frame around a door or window to create an eye-catching feature. A border frame will also look great set against a window or door moulding – either use the full border or cut a thin decorative strip to sit around the outside edge.
- Enhance a fireplace with a border surround – the perfect way to add extra interest to a decorative design or dress up a plain surround. If you don't want to go for a full frame, you could just use a single strip of border along the mantelpiece for emphasis.
- Break up the large plain expanse of wall beside a stairway with border frames, or use them to draw attention to architectural details such as dormers and soffits.
- If your bed doesn't have a headboard, use a border frame to create your own and make a stylish focal point in the bedroom.
- Add impact to a display of hanging pictures by framing them with borders.
- Border frames are a great way to offset mirrors and picture frames, and give a room a great feeling of depth. Allow at least 50 mm (2 in) of wall space between the frames and the border.

Specialist borders

Some companies produce specialist border papers, designed to create stunning feature walls and a variety of effects. Designed to simulate swathes of fabric, Classical columns and other architectural features, these look great combined with paper rosettes and bows. They can be arranged to form a border or hung in groups to emphasize a feature such as a fireplace, door, bedhead or an attractive piece of furniture.

You can also accentuate pretty picture frames or wall ornaments with specialist tassel and rope borders.

These designs are ideal for period homes, country style interiors or traditional schemes.

Design tricks

- Choose border colours carefully to suit the background. A contrasting scheme, using colours that sit opposite each other on the colour wheel, will make a dramatic impact, while a complementary scheme, combining colours that sit side by side, will be harmonious on the eye.
- Hang thick borders in a tall narrow room to draw the eye out and make the room seem wider.

▼ **below** Mix border shapes and textures for an eye-catching effect

PAPERING A FEATURE WALL OR ALCOVE

If you like the look of wallpaper but are wary of using it all over a room, use paper to highlight a feature wall or alcove instead. It's also a great way to experiment with a bolder pattern than you might otherwise go for. Keep the other walls simple with a single paint colour in a coordinating shade to offset the feature. There are also different techniques you can use on a feature wall to make the whole effect even more eye-catching. Try some of the following ideas to create a wow factor in a room.

Good idea

Tie several disjointed alcoves within a room together by papering them in the same paper. If you have painted alcoves, consider joining them together with a dramatic wallpaper border around the room, going into each alcove.

◀ **left** Leave a margin around the edge of a papered feature wall for an attractive finish

Papering an alcove

Finding the best starting point is the most important part of the job. The choice will be dictated by the size of the alcove and the paper's pattern. You should aim to have as few joins as possible within the alcove.

1 Measure the alcove to find the centre point, use a plumb line to create a vertical line on the wall (**diagram A**). Then either centre the first strip of paper over this line, or use the line as the joining point between two strips of paper. Generally, the former option will be the best one – so hang your centre piece of paper first, then paper to the left and to the right in that order.

2 Allow sufficient excess, about 100 mm (4 in), for trimming. Paste paper as normal, booking it and leaving the paste time to absorb if required.

3 Position the paper on the wall, and smooth into place. Trim along the bottom first (**diagram B**), then brush firmly into the curve of the alcove along the top with the bristles of your wallpapering brush (**diagram C**). Cut neatly with a knife.

Papering a feature wall

1 The point of a feature wall is that it needs to be seen to be appreciated, so make sure the wall you choose to highlight is the most eye-catching. If the room doesn't have an obvious focal point like a fireplace that naturally draws the eye, use the wall facing the door for visual impact. In a bedroom, the wall behind the headboard is the most obvious choice.

2 The papering technique is obviously the same as for papering a full room. However, as the idea is to create an eye-catching style feature within a room, it's important to plan carefully how you will hang the paper, particularly if using a bold pattern as you want to make sure it is displayed to best effect. The pattern will need to look balanced and so will need to be hung symmetrically.

3 As with papering an alcove, finding the best starting point is crucial. Use a measuring tape to find the centre point of the wall and draw a plumb line there. Now you have a choice to make. You can either centre your first strip of paper on this line or hang a strip of paper either side of it. This will probably be dictated by the pattern, ask yourself which method displays it to best effect.

4 If papering a chimney breast you will have to deal with papering around corners. Allow an overlap of 25 mm (1 in) at the angles. Don't try to work around a corner in one piece, as corners quite frequently are not square and the edge of the paper will move out of line. Bubbles and creases may also develop. For more information on papering around corners, see the relevant section in this book.

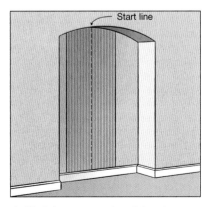

A Find the centre point of the alcove

B Trim along the bottom of the alcove

C Brush firmly into the curve

◄ **left** Make a feature in the bedroom with a pretty papered wall above the bed

Style tips

- Use bright colours and bold patterns to make a real style statement with a feature wall or alcove. Embossed papers and textured prints are also a good choice for features and alcoves.
- Pick up accents of the colour or pattern used in your feature wall with accessories. Cushions, throws, lampshades, pictures can all be coordinated with the key colours and patterns for a unified design scheme.
- If your feature wall has windows, opt for patterned curtains to match the wallpaper and really make an impact. This look works particularly well with pretty florals, toile de Jouy or stripes – and is ideal for a country style interior.
- Use bold retro prints for a dramatic look in a neutral design scheme – great for contemporary interiors.
- Create a striking effect by papering two facing walls in matching paper, paint the remaining walls in a coordinating shade.

Designer alternatives

Take inspiration from our suggestions, and create a feature wall with a difference for an even more eye-catching look.

- If the paper has a large pattern, cut out some of the patterns and frame them. Then hang them on the coordinating feature wall to add impact.
- Do not paper right to the edge of the wall, instead leave a margin all around the edge on all four sides to create a panelled effect that will make a real statement. This look works really well in a stylish living room either as a stand alone feature or to make an attractive backdrop for a stylish piece of furniture.
- Alternatively, if your bed doesn't have a headboard, use the panel effect to create a fabulous wallpaper 'headboard'. You could also create a layered effect in a contemporary bedroom, by making a wallpaper panel to sit behind the headboard.

PAPERING PANELS

Enhance wall panelling with wallpaper to add warmth, texture and depth to a design scheme. If you are not lucky enough to have real wood panelling in your home, consider making your own with decorative moulding. Create your own panels by covering large canvasses with bold patterned wallpaper.

◀ **left** Papered wall panels add texture and depth to an elegant living room

Designer tips

If painting the wall panels before papering, choose a shade that will complement the colours in your wallpaper. If your paper has a cream background for example, use cream – rather than white – on the panel surrounds.

Good idea

As well as papering within the panel, you could also paper between the panels for a really luxurious look. Use the same paper for a harmonized effect, or contrasting designs in complementary colours, to make a striking impact.

How to paper panels

1 Take a careful measurement of the panel's interior dimensions and transfer these measurements, using a pencil and ruler, to the back of the roll of wallpaper. Use a spirit level to ensure the lines are straight.

2 Now you have two choices. You can either cut the piece accurately to size, or leave a margin of about 75 mm (3 in) all around and trim the paper once it is pasted to the wall.

3 Paste according to the manufacturer's instructions, taking care to paste right out to the edges to ensure the paper doesn't lift or curl. Make sure the paste is suitable for both the paper and the wall surface to which you are attaching it.

4 Fix paper securely to the wall, lining up the edges with the pencil marks and smoothing into place with a brush, taking care to remove any air bubbles. If you have over-cut the panel, use the back edge of the scissors to run along the paper along the sides of the moulding. Pull back slightly from the wall and cut the excess along the crease line (**diagram A**). Then smooth the paper back into position with the brush.

Alternatively you could use a trimming knife but be careful not to damage the panels.

5 Using a damp cloth or sponge, clean the paste carefully off the mouldings afterwards to prevent marks or stains occurring.

▲ **above** Create your own panelling by covering wooden boards cut to size with patterned wallpaper

Designer trick

Many DIY retailers sell pre-cut wooden panels made from wooden moulding – just stick to the wall with 'grip fix' or other strong adhesive.

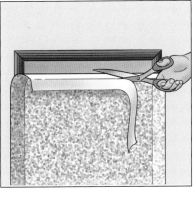

A Cut the excess along the crease

Make your own

Use quadrant wood, available from any builder's suppliers, to make your own wood panelling. Saw to the lengths required and screw to the wall, using filler to plug the holes afterwards. Sand and mitre the ends at each corner. Paint in the colour required before papering.

Alternatively hang the paper first, then fix the panel around the edges, attaching securely to the wall.

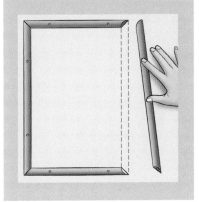

PAPERING BENEATH A DADO OR PICTURE RAIL

Dado refers to the wall space between the chair (or dado) rail, half way up the wall and the skirting board. Traditionally this part of the wall was given a decorative or protective treatment to a height of three to four feet, topped by a moulding called the dado rail. In the Edwardian period the dado was replaced in popularity by the picture rail, and both architectural features are still very popular today.

◀ **left** A large room can be made warm and inviting by papering up to the picture rail and then painting the wall above the same colour as the ceiling

◀ **far left** Team traditional florals with white panelling to create an elegant living space

Design

Wallpaper, used above the dado rail, below it or on both parts of the wall, is an ideal way of highlighting this feature. In the Victorian period, heavily patterned flock and velvet wallpapers in rich luxurious colours like deep green and burgundy were very much in fashion and used above the dado rail. Designs were complicated and geometric patterns in particular were very popular.

However, as trends moved toward lighter, simpler designs, the dado was removed. The focus of the wall now moved up to picture rail height and murals, both stencilled and painted just below the ceiling level, became popular in the Edwardian period. Today, papering beneath a picture rail and painting above is a clever way of making a large room cosier and more inviting.

Techniques

The technique employed in papering above or beneath a dado rail is the same as papering a full room, except you are working with shorter strips of paper. This makes it slightly easier for a beginner to hang, particularly if papering the lower half of the wall as there will be no need for stepladders. It's also a job easily accomplished by one person.

Remember to leave enough paper for trimming at both the top and the bottom of the strip. Make sure when trimmed directly underneath the dado rail that you do not damage it with sharp blades – it may be best to trim with a scissors.

Carefully remove any splashes of paste that end up on the dado rail or panelling as you work – they may stain if left on too long.

Style tricks

Add a dado rail to a wall in a modern home to create architectural interest. Dado rails are easy to attach, just saw to size, remembering to mitre interior and exterior corners, drill and screw into place. Then plug the screw holes with filler before sanding and painting. This creates an immediate eye-catching feature, which can be enhanced by coordinating or contrasting papers.

Alternatively, attach a wallpaper border at dado rail height all around the room, and use different papers above and beneath. Use a border that is created to look like moulding for an even more authentic touch. Add the border after you have finished papering the walls as this will cover the join between papers for a seamless finish.

Good ideas

- Cheat and buy a dado kit, available from most DIY retailers. Pre-cut lengths of rail come with pre-cut joins, the fast way to create perfectly mitred corners and a stylish finish to a room.

- It is easy to attach a dado rail to a wall using 'grip fix' or other adhesive but never glue a dado over existing wallpaper – its weight could pull the paper off the wall!

- Give a traditional dado a contemporary makeover by spraying with gold or silver paint and teaming with a contemporary metallic paper underneath the railing.

▶ **right** A hardworking embossed paper is an ideal choice for the wall beneath a dado rail. It can also be painted to match the rest of the room

◀ **left** Here wallpaper with a wide stripe really makes an impact and adds texture when used beneath a dado rail

USING TWO DIFFERENT PAPERS IN ONE ROOM SCHEME

Combining two papers within one room is a very effective design trick and works well with a large variety of styles and looks. The key is to know what works well together and how to use it to best effect, so select your papers carefully. There are some basic design guidelines to follow – stick to these and you can't go wrong. The finished look can be formal and elegant, warm and welcoming or cutting edge fashionable – the choice is endless and it all depends on the papers you choose.

Choosing papers: Hints and tips

There are a number of ways to mix papers. There's no point choosing papers that look great individually, but don't work well together. To ensure you get a good blend there are a few tricks you can employ.

- Choose two papers with the same pattern, but in different colourways. The colours can either coordinate or contrast, it depends on how bold you want the finished effect to be.
- Opt for papers with different patterns, for example a floral print and a striped design, but blend the look together by making sure both papers use the same or similar colourways.
- Choose papers that have different patterns but are slight variations on one colour – for example two different shades of blue. This tonal colour matching will also have the effect of making a small room feel more spacious, as the eye can move through the room easily without obstruction, making the room seem bigger.
- Select papers from the same paper family. Check out pattern books at wallpaper stores – complementary papers sit together in these books to make choosing easy.

◀ **left** Bold wallpaper designs are mixed easily here by using the same pattern in different colours

▲ **above** Make use of a dado rail to display contrasting florals and stripes

Design tricks

The room's dimensions and layout will influence how you mix papers within the space. A feature such as a dado rail, creates a natural division for your papers – use one above and the second below.

In a contemporary home you could use one paper to create a stylish feature wall and cover the remaining walls in the second paper. Or make an eye-catching feature by using paper on two adjoining walls, and paint the rest of the room. In both cases, change the paper at the corners, when papering floor to ceiling.

▲ **above** Section a room into easily definable spaces using different wallpapers

Style advice

- Use different papers to segment rooms – both large and small – and suggest different 'spaces', for example a work or study area in a bedroom or living room, a dining area in a kitchen, a dressing area in a large bathroom or bedroom.
- Create a stunning feature wall by using one paper to make a dramatic centre panel, fixing the second paper at each side of the panel. This works very well with large bold patterns like florals and stripes, or contrasting geometric designs.
- Remember to keep things in perspective when choosing your papers, if you opt for a large floral, team it with a large stripe, scale should be consistent so that the papers will work together.
- Formal papers with geometric or embossed designs, teamed with luxurious tones such as rich golds, reds and greens, will look good in period homes and elegant living spaces. Keep colours light and avoid small detailed patterns in contemporary homes, florals suit country style interiors – a small floral print looks great with a thin stripe.

▶ **right** Mix a wide contemporary stripe with a traditional flock for dramatic impact

Good idea

Using two papers on one wall is a great way to break up the dominating effect of a very high wall, and make it seem shorter. This will cosy up a large space that might otherwise feel rather cold.

PAPERING THE PANELS OF A DOOR OR WARDROB

Use wallpaper on furniture to introduce accents of colour around the room – it's quickly and easily done, as well as being a great way to use up wallpaper remnants. Wallpaper is so versatile and suitable for covering a wide variety of surfaces, from door and wardrobe panels to lamps and dressing tables.

◀ **left** Add the pefect finishing touch by papering behind shelving and inside cupboards

Papering panels

If you have a panelled door or wardrobe, give it an instant facelift and add some colour and pattern by papering the panels with wallpaper. It's simple to do and will instantly brighten up your room. Choose pretty florals for a feminine touch or a bold pattern to make a statement.

1 First prepare the surface by washing with a sugar soap to clean thoroughly. If working with a glossy surface, lightly rub down with a fine grade sandpaper first.

2 Select which part of the wallpaper pattern you want to display. Measure the panels and transfer the measurements to the back of the wallpaper using a pencil and ruler, ensuring the selected pattern is displayed to best advantage within these dimensions (**diagram A**). Cut the other panels to match, or choose a random match for an alternative effect. Use a spirit level when drawing the lines to ensure they are perfectly straight.

3 Cut panels using either a sharp scissors or a blade and the edge of a steel rule. You can either cut the pieces exactly to size, or leave a margin of about 75 mm (3 in) all around for trimming once the paper is fixed to the panel.

4 Paste according to the manufacturer's instructions, taking care to paste right out to the edges to prevent panels lifting or curling. Make sure the paste is suitable for both the paper and surface of the door or wardrobe.

5 Attach the paper to the panel, smoothing into place with a brush to remove wrinkles and air bubbles.

6 If you have cut to fit, ensure the edges of the paper line up neatly with the sides of the panel – if not, peel off and refit.

7 If you have over-cut the panel, use the back edge of a scissors or bristle brush to run along the paper along the sides of the moulding. Pull back slightly and trim off the excess along the crease line using a sharp scissors. Then smooth the paper back into position with the brush. Alternatively you could use a trimming knife but be careful not to damage the panels.

8 Clean the paste carefully off the sides of the panels afterwards to prevent marks or stains occurring.

Papering inside cabinets

As well as lining cabinet shelves with wallpaper, you could also paper the back of the cabinet for a real country cottage effect. This look would work equally well with open shelving or bookcases, where the supporting wall or back panel is papered as well as the shelves.

1 Measure the shelves carefully and then transfer these measurements to the wallpaper using a ruler and pencil. Use a spirit level to keep the lines straight.

2 Cut the pieces to size and attach to the shelves, using paste that is suitable for both the paper and the surface it is being attached to (**diagram B**).

3 Smooth into place with a brush to remove wrinkles and air bubbles.

4 Measure the area behind shelves and, as before, transfer the measurements to the wallpaper using a ruler and pencil. Follow the steps above to complete the job.

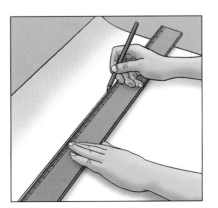

A Transfer the measurements

B Paste the paper onto the shelves

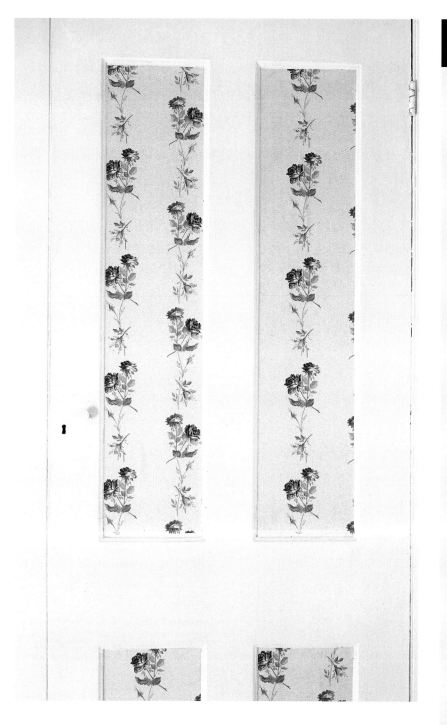

Great ideas

As well as door panels and shelving, wallpaper can be used in a variety of ways around a room to add colour and texture. Use our tips below for inspiration – a great way to add flashes of pattern to a room, even for the non-converted!

- Glam up a dressing table or beside locker by covering a lampshade and base in wallpaper to make an eye-catching display. For the perfect finishing touch, cover a few of your favourite books in matching paper and pile alongside.

- Mount wallpaper onto a plain wooden screen to create a stylish private dressing area. Use a bold pattern to make a statement, or a pretty floral motif for an effect that is very feminine.

- Cover shoeboxes with paper and pile on top of a wardrobe or bedside cabinet for a pretty splash of colour – great for hiding clutter too.

- Fit a sheet of wallpaper to the top of a dressing or occasional table in a bedroom or living room, and place a sheet of glass on top to protect – a glazier will be able to cut it to whatever size you require. There is no need to glue or paste the paper to the surface as the glass will hold it firmly in place, so you can update the look quickly and easily by changing the paper whenever you like.

▲ **above** Add texture and visual interest by papering door panels

▶ **right** Use contrasting papers on a cupboard or wardrobe for a look that is feminine and fresh

GLOSSARY

Use this handy at-a-glance guide to sort your butt joints from your double-cut seams and find out what's what in the world of wallpaper.

Accent wall Also known as a feature wall, this wall is a key focal point in a room, given a special design emphasis to make it stand out from the other walls. It is generally the first wall you see when you walk into a room.

All-over pattern A pattern that is distributed evenly over the surface of the wall covering.

Anaglypta A heavy embossed wall covering that can be painted after hanging.

Bob line A tool used to mark a perfectly straight vertical line on the wall, used as an aid to hanging wallpaper in straight lines. Also known as a plumb line.

Booking The technique of folding the top and bottom of a strip of wallpaper to the centre after pasting in order to make it easier to carry to the wall and to give the paste a chance to soak into the paper.

Border A decorative strip of wallpaper used to provide an attractive finish and add architectural interest. Commonly hung at ceiling, picture or dado rail height, borders can also be used independently to create a variety of effects.

Broad knife Wide knife used as a trim guide, may also be used for removing old wallpaper from walls.

Bulldog paper clips Clips to fasten paper firmly to the table so it doesn't roll up while pasting.

Butt join or seam Neatly aligned joins that occur when wallpaper strips are fitted edge to edge without overlapping.

Chair rail Decorative wooden moulding fixed at half wall height, also known as a dado rail.

Chintz A paper that resembles brightly coloured printed cotton material.

Clay paste Used for hanging specialist papers such as lincrusta.

Colourway The combination of colours in a design.

Coordinating papers Papers that complement each other due to pattern similarities in colour and design, used to best effect above and below a dado, on adjoining walls or in adjoining rooms.

Cork glasspaper block A small block of cork, around which sandpaper can be wrapped to make it easier to grip when sanding surfaces.

Dado The wall space between the chair rail and the skirting board.

Dado rail Decorative wooden moulding fixed at half wall height, also known as a chair rail.

Dado paper Wall covering that covers the lower part of the wall or dado.

Diagonal pattern A pattern that runs at a slant, in a diagonal formation.

Directional print A pattern that needs to be hung in a particular direction, such as flowers that 'grow' up the wall.

Double cutting A technique used to achieve a perfectly fitted seam on papers that do not need matching. Strips are overlapped about 75 mm (3 in) and a sharp blade is used to cut through both layers. Then the top strip is peeled back, the bottom strip peeled off and the top brushed back against the wall.

Drop match Also known as offset match, this pattern runs diagonally across the wall, and the pattern in every other strip is the same at the ceiling line. The edges of this paper will be different on each side, with motifs staggered between the drops.

Dry hanging This involves pasting the wall rather than the back of the wall covering.

Dye lot A number printed on the label of every roll of wallpaper, also known as the run. It refers to a batch of wallpaper rolls printed or 'run' at the same time, in which colours will be perfectly consistent. All rolls used in a room should be from the same dye lot.

Embossed paper A paper with a raised or textured surface, created by pressing a design into the back of the paper during manufacture.

Feature wall Also known as an accent wall, this wall is a key focal point in a room, given a special design emphasis to make it stand out from the other walls.

Felt wallpaper roller Used instead of a seam roller to smooth down edges after hanging when working with grasscloths, flocks and heavily embossed papers.

Fill Area between the chair rail and frieze of a wall, also known as the sidewall.

Foil Also known as metallic, this paper has a sheen to simulate the look of metal.

Flocked paper With a raised pattern that is soft to the touch, flocked paper is created by bonding tiny fibres onto the surface to give the look of velvet.

Free match A continuous pattern that doesn't need matching.

Frieze Traditionally a pictorial border, running around the room above door height.

Geometric prints Also known as horizontal line prints, these include stripes, plaids and checks.

Georgian Period style encompassing the reigns of George I, II and III in England during the period 1714 to 1795.

Inside corner A conventional corner, formed where two adjoining walls meet.

Jacobean A style developed from Tudor and Elizabethan styles.

Lincrusta A heavy wall covering, dating from the 1800s and featuring a raised design surface with the texture of hard putty. Can be painted after hanging.

Lining paper A plain paper used underneath the main paper to provide a smooth surface on imperfect walls or as a good base for heavier papers; available in different weights and grades.

Medallion A round, square, oval or rectangular decoration, commonly used with borders to hide joins and create a decorative effect.

Metallic Also known as foil, this paper has a sheen to simulate the look of metal.

Motif The recurring design or subject matter of a wallpaper pattern.

Offset match Also known as drop match, this pattern runs diagonally across the wall, and the pattern in every other strip is the same at the ceiling line. The edges of this paper will be different on each side, with motifs staggered between the drops.

Outside corner A corner formed, when two walls, not facing each other, are joined.

Paperhanging brush A large soft-bristle brush used to smooth paper into place after fixing on the wall to remove wrinkles and air bubbles.

Pattern matching Joining strips of wallpaper so the pattern lines up correctly, a process that is dictated by the pattern itself. There are four basic types of pattern – free, straight, offset/drop and random/plain match. See individual entries for information.

Pattern repeat The length of a pattern before it repeats.

Peelable paper Easy to remove for redecoration, peelable papers usually come off the wall in a few layers.

Plaid Designs consisting of crossed stripes, originating in Scottish tartans.

Plumb line A tool used to mark a perfectly straight vertical line on the wall, used as an aid to hanging wallpaper in straight lines. Also known as a bob line.

Prepasted paper A wall covering that comes with paste already applied to the back, which is soaked in water to activate before hanging.

Primer Also known as sealer, primer creates a non-porous surface that seals new walls and makes wallpaper easier to remove afterwards.

Railroading Hanging a paper horizontally rather than vertically, often used for lining papers.

Random or plain match This type of pattern varies according to paper design. For example, a textured match will look better if each length is hung the opposite way up.

Regency English period, lasting from approximately 1793 to 1820.

Relief cut Cut made in an inside corner or at a window casing, moulding or other protrusion to relieve pressure on a large sheet of paper and allow it to lie flat against the wall.

Reverse hanging Technique of alternately hanging strips right way up and upside down, dictated by certain random patterns.

Run A number printed on the label of every roll of wallpaper, also known as the dye lot. It refers to a batch of wallpaper rolls printed or 'run' at the same time, in which colours will be perfectly consistent. All rolls used in a room should be from the same run.

Sanding block Block of sandpaper, which offers an easy grip for sanding.

Scrubbable This paper can be wiped clean and, as it is stronger than washable paper, will withstand more vigorous cleaning.

Sealer Also known as primer, primer creates a non-porous surface that seals new walls and makes wallpaper easier to remove afterwards.

Seam Area where two wallpaper strips are joined.

Seam roller A tool used to smooth down wallpaper edges when the paste is nearly dry to make sure they are firmly attached to the wall. Not suitable for use on grasscloths, flocks and heavily embossed papers.

Sidewall Area between the chair rail and frieze of a wall, also known as the fill.

Sizing A powder mixed with water and applied to a painted or sealed surface to make the surface tacky and ensure the paper will adhere better.

Small scale pattern A small design repeat, usually spaced close together.

Soffit The underside of an architectural feature, such as an arch.

Sponge Vital piece of wallpaper kit, used for cleaning paste from the paper surface, mouldings and skirting boards when hanging.

Straight edge A ruler or other tool used as a guide for a blade when trimming wallpaper along edges.

Strip Length of wall covering, cut to fit the height of the area being papered.

Strippable Easy to remove for redecoration, this paper pulls away from the wall in one piece.

Sugar soap A substance mixed with water to create a cleaning solution to remove dirt and grease from walls before papering.

Surface printing A conventional form of wallpaper printing where the design is raised on the roller and transferred to the paper.

Swag A looped or swinging design, usually comprising garlands, leaves, ribbons and other drapery.

Swatch Sample

Straight match This paper has the same pattern running down both edges, and the pattern continues directly across the strips. The same part of the pattern is always the same distance from the ceiling in every strip.

Toile de Jouy Highly decorative engraving-like print of landscape and figure motifs which originated in the town of Jouy in France in the 18th century.

Top colours The colours that form the design against the background colour.

Trestles and scaffold boards Materials to construct a secure platform, ideal for wallpapering ceilings.

Trimming The process of removing excess paper along ceilings, skirting boards, windows, doors and other obstacles.

Tromp l'oeil From the French 'fool the eye', this design creates a three dimensional illusion by means of shadow and graphic textures.

Unpasted paper Conventional wallpaper that requires pasting with a suitable adhesive before hanging.

Vinyl A tough, hardwearing plastic-coated paper, which is washable and particularly suited for kitchens and bathrooms.

Vinyl coated With a thin skin of plastic, its protective surface makes it suitable for kitchens and bathrooms and it is easier to remove than standard vinyl.

Washable A durable, easy-care paper with a thin plastic coating that can be regularly wiped down.

Wet hanging The conventional way of hanging wallpaper that involves pasting the back of each strip before hanging.

USEFUL ADDRESSES

UK

Anaglypta and Lincrusta
The Imperial House Décor Group
 (UK) Ltd
Belgrave Mills
Belgrave Road
Darwen
Lancashire
BB3 2RR

Anna French
108 Shakespeare Road
London
SE24 0QW
www.annafrench.co.uk

Baer & Ingram
Dragon Works
Leigh on Mendip
Radstock
BA3 5QZ
www.baer-ingram.co.uk

Cole and Son (Wallpapers) Ltd
Ground Floor 10
Chelsea Harbour Design Centre
Lots Road
London
SW10 0XE
www.cole-and-son.com

Fun To See™ Ltd
14 Compton Place
Eastbourne
East Sussex
BN20 8AB
www.funtosee.com

Harlequin
Ladybird House
Beeeches Road
Loughborough
Leistershire
LE11 2HA

Homebase Limited
Avebury
489–499 Avebury Boulevard
Saxon Gate West
Central Milton Keynes
Bucks
MK9 2NW
www.homebase.co.uk

Jane Churchill
110 Fulham Road
London
SW3 6HU
www.janechurchill.com

Laura Ashley Ltd
27 Bagleys Lane
Fulham
London
SW6 2QA
www.lauraashley.com

Squigee
Unit 25E
Glasgow
G13 1EU
www.squigee.com

Today Interiors Ltd
Hollis Road
Grantham
Lincolnshire
NG31 7QH
www.today-interiors.co.uk

Timorous Beasties
384 Great Western Rd
Glasgow
G4 9HT UK.
www.timorousbeasties.com

Watts of Westminster
3/14 Third Floor
Centre Dome
Chelsea Harbour Design Centre
London
SW10 0EX
www.wattsofwestminster.com

USA

By Design
2419 E. Perkins Ave.
Sandusky
Ohio 44870-7992

Habitat Wallpaper & Blinds
2070A N Clybourn Ave.
Chicago
Illinois 60614

Manchester Paint & Wallpaper
185 Middle Tpke W
Manchester
Conneticut 06040

Sipersteins
415 Montgomery Street
Jersey City
New Jersey 07302

Wallpapers to Go
23812 Via Fabricante
Suite A-4
Mission Viejo
California 92691
www.wallpaperstogo.com

Wallpapers to Go
9311 Katy Freeway
Houston
Texas 77024

Wallpapers to Go
2525 West Anderson Lane
Austin
Texas 78757

Wallpapers to Go
8518 East 71st Street
Tulsa
Olklahoma 74133

Internet resources
www.wallpaperstore.com
www.usawallpaper.com

INDEX

ACKNOWLEDGEMENTS

Many thanks to the following companies and individuals for lending images to be used in this book:

Anaglypta (Imperial Home Décor Group UK Ltd) 6, 17 top, 83, 86; **Baer & Ingram** 52; **Simon Bevan/Homes and Gardens/IPC Syndication** 79; **Jane Churchill** 22, 62 top, 88 main; **Cole & Son (Wallpapers) Ltd** 15 top, 15 bottom, 18, 34, 78 main; **Fun To See** 68-71; **Martin Gould** 36, 48 main; **Harlequin Fabrics and Wallcoverings** 2, 7, 8, 10, 19 bottom, 20, 21, 23, 62 main, 63, 82, 84 main; **Homebase** 44 top, 58 main, 90, 91; **Lincrusta (Imperial Home Décor Group UK Ltd)** 14, 61, 66 main, 67, 78 top; **Monkwell Furnishing Fabrics and Wallpapers** 45; **Nono Designs** 75 main; **Lizzie Orme/Country Homes and Interiors/IPC Syndication** 44 main, 65; **Ornamenta** 39, 72 main, 73; **Jeremy Phillips/25 Beautiful Homes/IPC Syndication** 56; **Richard's Wallcoverings and Fabrics** 16 bottom; **Squigee (Today Interiors Ltd)** 4, 5, 9, 42, 17 bottom, 33, 47, 77; **Lucinda Symons/Country Home & Interiors/IPC Syndication** 19 top; **Tektura Plc** 40, 55; **Today Interiors Ltd** 30, 58 top, 64, 80 main, 81, 85, 87; **Debi Treloar/Homes and Gardens/IPC Syndication** 28; **Simon Whitmore/Ideal Home/IPC Syndication** 50; **Walls of the Wild** 16 top; **Shona Wood** 13; **Tim Young/Homes and Gardens/IPC Syndication** 49; **PSC/Ideal Home/IPC Syndication** 53

The wallpaper symbols on page 25 are reproduced with permission from the **British Standards Institution (BSI)**.